Dedicated to Norma and our two children, Sue and Tom, and in tribute to my parents, John F. Voth and Helena Hildebrandt-Voth, who never returned to the land of their fathers but who made it possible for me to do so and to see the world realistically and with appreciation.

Preface

Israel joined the family of nations in the tumultuous Cold War year of 1948. Ironically, the United States and the Soviet Union, rival leaders in the Cold War, agreed on a common policy to create a Jewish state in Palestine in the face of sharp opposition from Arab nationalists and uneasiness in the British Foreign Office.

This book gives a detailed account of how Soviet policy turned the proverbial 180 degrees. It presents the rising crescendo of conflict between Soviet and Israeli interests—set against the background of increasing Soviet enticement with Arab nationalism. Stemming from the Moscow's desire to replace Western control with its own dominance, a chain of events was set in motion which resulted in the complete reversal of Soviet Middle East policy from supporting Israel against the Arabs, to supporting the Arabs against Israel. Our Middle East story, however, could not be adequately told without an account of the wider international political events having an impact on that area during these crucial ten years when the Soviet reversal took place. A knowledge of the post-World War II roles of the super-powers as related to the Middle East is essential to an understanding of the contemporary Arab Muslim world. The material of this book is intended to be vital to that knowledge.

Our account of this decade-long drama in the Middle East is divided into two parts: the first discusses the pro-Israel period of Soviet policy; the second traces the increasing tensions in the Soviet Union's relations with Israel leading eventually to the strongly anti-Israel, pro-Arab foreign policy effectively in place by 1956. Singled out for special attention are seven major national leaders who played important roles in the drama as it unfolded on the international stage. The biographical sketches of these heroes, or villains, will hopefully add to the reader's understanding and interest in the crucial decade.

I wish to give special recognition and appreciation to Dr. Ishaq Ghanayem for invaluable scholarly contributions to the book. He was one of my graduate students at San Jose University during the early stages of the project. He later transferred to the University of California, Santa Barbara, for his doctoral studies and has become a recognized scholar on Henry Kissinger's work in the Nixon and Ford administrations.

Among the many others deserving special appreciation are Robert B. Harmon and Milton Loventhal of the professional library staff who read the manuscript and offered invaluable suggestions; Tom Carter, also of the SJSU library staff, was extremely helpful in efficiently making the resources of the library available to me. My professional colleagues of the SJSU faculty, Drs. Charles Burdick and Michael Boll, deserve a special thanks for reading the manuscript and sharing ideas in the areas of their special expertise.

My special thanks are also given to my wife, Norma, a published writer in her own field of endeavor, who contributed invaluable patience, editing skills, and innumerable other tasks to make the book possible.

I also wish to express appreciation to Bernard Scheier, Mary-Lynne Tupper, and Tom Holmes for "going above and beyond the call of duty" to help make the book a reality.

Alden H. Voth

Contents

Part I:

The Pro-Israel Period

Introduction

The strong Soviet support of Arab states against Israel after the mid-1950s has caused many to forget Russia's role in the creation of Israel. The Soviet Union was consistently more supportive of Israel's birth in the United Nations debates than was the United States. Perhaps the most Zionist speech ever presented by a big power in the United Nations General Assembly was made by Mr. Andrei Gromyko on November 26, 1947. The Soviet representative, *inter alia,* said:

> The representatives of the Arab States claim that the partition of Palestine would be an historic injustice. But this view of the case is unacceptable. ... The Jewish people has been closely lined with Palestine for a considerable period in history ... We must not overlook the position in which the Jewish people found themselves as a result of the recent war. ... As a result of the war which was unleashed by Hitlerite Germany, the Jews, as a people, have suffered more than any other. ... There was not a single country in Western Europe which succeeded in adequately protecting the interests of the Jewish people against the arbitrary acts and violence of the Hitlerites. ...

> The delegation of the USSR maintains that the decision to partition Palestine is in keeping with the high principles and aims of the United Nations. It is in keeping with the principle of the national self-determination of peoples. ...

> The USSR delegation, unlike some other delegations, has from the outset taken a clear-cut definite and unequivocal stand

in this matter. It is consistently maintaining this stand. It has no intention of maneuvering and manipulating votes as unfortunately is done at the Assembly, especially in connexion [sic] with the consideration of the Palestinian question.[1]

Later, after the proclamation of the independent state of Israel on May 14, 1948, and after the national armies of the surrounding Arab states invaded Israel, the Soviet delegate, Andrei Gromyko, again took the floor in the Security Council to charge the Arab states with violating the May 22 Security Council cease-fire resolution.[2] In contrast to the vituperative charges against Israel beginning a half decade later, the Soviet representative at this time overtly charged the Arab states with an organized invasion of Palestine, and specifically referred to "the new Jewish State" as "the victim of aggression."[3]

This position represented an interesting turn of events. During World War II the Soviet Union abandoned its criticism of Zionism as a form of nationalism associated with the decadent world of capitalism. Shortly after the war, in 1946, the Soviet government briefly criticized Zionism for encouraging the Jews to leave Europe and supporting the continuation of the British-controlled Mandate of Palestine. The Arabs, in contrast, were in this single case referred to as progressive in leadership. Said the Soviet spokesman, "The Palestine problem cannot be resolved by imperialist means. The majority of the population regards the country as an Arab country . . ."[4]

A year later, however, the Arabs were criticized as reactionary and the Jews of Palestine received favorable press treatment. This crescendo of Soviet support for the Yishuv (the Jewish community in Palestine) reached its peak when the UN General Assembly passed the resolution in support of an independent Jewish state in Palestine. At the time, Soviet leaders became outspoken competitors with the United States for claims of being more supportive of Israel. Representatives of the Soviet Union made public claims of more genuine and consistent backing for the Jews in Palestine than what they characterized as the vacillation and pretentiousness of the United States. Attention was also called to the *de facto* nature of American recognition whereas the Soviet Union had extended the more prestigious *de jure* recognition of Israel.[5]

NOTES

1. *United Nations Official Records*, Plenary Meetings of the General Assembly (Verbatim Records), Vol. II, 125th Meeting, November 26, 1947, pp. 1358–63.

2. United Nations Security Council, *Official Records, Third Year, Supplement for May, 1948*, Document S/773.

3. United Nations Security Council, *Official Records, 309th and 310th Meetings*, 309th Meeting, 29 May 1948.

4. See, for instance; V. B. Lutskii, *Palestinskaia Problema*, Moscow, 1946, pp. 28ff.

5. See publications such as: (1) V. B. Lutskii, *Angliiskii i Amerikanskii Imperialism na Blizhnem*, Moscow, 1948, p. 27. (2) *Novoe Vremia*, September 30, 1948.

CHAPTER 1:

British Middle East Policy and the Soviet Reaction

After World War I, British foreign policy was designed to promote its imperial influence in the Middle East by the use of the House of Hashim—Hussein ibn Ali, the Grand Sherif of Mecca, and three of his sons, Ali, Abdullah, and Feisal. It was to be what Winston Churchill referred to as the "Sherifian solution" to the post-war political reconstruction for the British in the Middle East.

The French intolerance of Feisal's authority at Damascus, and Abdel Aziz ibn Saud's success in driving the Hashimites from Arabia eliminated a great deal of the British policy projections.

Immediately after V-E Day the British seemed, again, to be in a favorable position of influence in the Middle East—or so it appeared. France's position in the Middle East had eroded badly by the end of World War II.

Soviet Involvement

The Soviet Union, in contrast to World War I, now also entered the Middle East picture. Even before V-E Day, the victorious sweep of Soviet arms had put the Western allies on notice that concessions in the Middle East would be expected. However, a study of the crucial background of Palestine politics is best seen through a focus on the British, and an important facet of this drama involved world Jewry.

7

Zionists Confront Britain on Palestine

Immediately after the war, the British had to face the Zionists' wrath. The Jews vehemently opposed the British anti-Jewish war policy which they felt would callously be continued if pressure were not mounted to stop it. Before the war, beginning at the time of the infamous Munich appeasement in fall, 1938, the Colonial Secretary, Malcom MacDonald, took the initiative in decisively moving foreign policy into an anti-Zionist, pro-Arab stance. This shift evolved into the London Round Table Conference (Feb. 7 to March 12, 1939) and the official statement of British policy in the White Paper of May 17 (1939). MacDonald frankly reminded the concerned Jewish leadership of their eroded bargaining position relative to the escalated political clout which the Arabs had gratuitously received by the fact of the dangerously destabilizing international situation.

British national interests could now ignore Jewish feelings since world Jewry was essentially locked into a pro-Allied position given the treatment the Jews were receiving by Nazi Germany. On the other hand, given the deteriorating international situation caused by threatened German expansion, it was imperative that Britain insure itself against alienating the Arab Middle East—British national interests demanded a pro-Arab Palestine position at the expense of the Jews. This was spelled out in the 1939 White Paper.

Some effort was made by Germany to exploit this explosive latent conflict during the war. The Jews organized an "underground railroad" to smuggle their persecuted kin to Palestine. According to Howard Sachar, "the Germans themselves encouraged it. They handed the Jews down the Danube to Rumanian ports; the refugees were then shipped off in discarded freighters or cattle boats. The British viewed this traffic as a kind of 'fifth column'—one that ideally fostered the Nazi purpose of arousing Arabs and undermining the security of Palestine."[1]

Regardless of how tragic this situation appeared to the Jews, the British insisted on their Palestine policy of doing nothing which would antagonize the Arabs. In November, 1940, the British loaded 1,900 East European Jews—caught trying to get into Palestine—on the *Patria* for forced shipment to Mauritius Island in the Indian Ocean. Haganah, the Jewish underground army, was determined to halt the operation even at the cost of innocent human life of its own people. Other similar British acts also resulted in similar tragedies for the Jews.

The British ran into trouble with their efforts at rebuilding the post-war Middle East political order on the continuation of its pro-Arab war policy. What was possible during the war did not work for the British after the war. The British-Zionist conflict became a challenge which would be utilized by the Soviet Union for its own interests. At the end of World War II, the British military position in the Middle East appeared much stronger than, in reality, it was. The British national economy, upon which a modern military force rests, was a hollow shell. The military bases in both Egypt and Iraq were being eroded as a viable defense asset by increasingly serious nationalist agitation against the unequal treaties. In Palestine the British faced an awesome challenge from Jewish terrorists who were determined to make the 1939 White Paper policy too costly to maintain.

The New Labor Government in Britain

The British Labor Party's victory in the July, 1945, elections was hailed by the Zionists as a real bonus (although Winston Churchill, as head of the Conservative Party, was a man of considerable pro-Zionist sympathy). In opposition, the Labor Party had taken a pro-Zionist position which was domestically quite popular as long as, being out of power, it didn't have to face up to the responsibility of that policy.

Ernest Bevin

Ernest Bevin in 1941 after Prime Minister Winston Churchill had appointed him Minister of Labor and National Service in the War Cabinet. After the German surrender in World War II, Bevin was appointed Foreign Secretary in the new Labor Government. (Courtesy, Library of Congress)

Ernest Bevin was born in the English village of Winsford, Somersetshire, March 9, 1881, the son of a landless farm laborer who died four months before the infant Ernest arrived in this world. Until his mother died, he found himself in an outspoken, compulsive Methodist religious environment. Orphaned at age six, Ernest Bevin went to live with his sister where he was able to attend school through the fourth grade before being sent to work on a farm for wages which amounted to little more than board and room. The young Bevin left shortly for the city and became deeply involved in the British labor movement.

His early claim to recognition was as a labor organizer and successful advocate of labor union mergers to gain more bargaining power. During World War I he accepted Prime Minister David Lloyd George's invitation to expedite military supply shipping to the British Expeditionary Forces in France by becoming a member of the government's Port and Transit Executive Committee.

In the post-World War I period, the now recognized labor leader succeeded in forming the Transportation and General Workers' Union from almost two dozen smaller independent unions. Later, this union grew in membership to the point where it was considered the largest labor union in the world. Bevin was elected general secretary of the TGWU. He was one of the organizers of Britain's General Strike in 1926. In October, 1937, Bevin was elected chairman of the Trades Union Congress.

His government career began in 1940 when Winston Churchill appointed him Minister of Labor and National Service in the War Cabinet. The Labor Party's success in the July, 1945, elections (in the middle of the Potsdam summit conference) brought that Party to power, and Anthony Eden was replaced by Ernest Bevin as Foreign Secretary. Bevin had originally preferred the position of Chancellor of the Exchequer, but Winston Churchill and King George VI both encouraged the new Prime Minister, Clement

Attlee, to have Bevin take charge of foreign affairs, where a strong personality was important to stand up to the post-war Soviet demands.

Ernest Bevin came under considerable criticism for his Middle East policy. The Labor Party had campaigned on a platform supporting the creation of a Jewish state in Palestine. Once in power, Bevin was converted by the professionals in the Foreign Office to an anti-partition, pro-Arab policy for Palestine. He came to believe that a British post-war Middle East policy could best be built upon the pre-war record of friendship with the essentially pro-Western Arabs. The Jews were a religious grouping, not a nation as were the Arabs. Giving way to Jewish aspirations would be disruptive and tend to weaken the Western position in the Middle East.

On October 10, 1945, the most effective Zionist spokesman, Chaim Weizmann, had an appointment with Bevin, who gave him a chilling reception. The following month (on November 13, 1945) the Foreign Secretary re-affirmed the essentials of the anti-Jewish White Paper of 1939 embodying the stipulations of no partition, very limited Jewish immigration, and essentially a freeze on the Jews' right to buy land in Palestine. This was totally unacceptable to the Jews. It was also opposed by the United States, which requested Britain to allow for the immediate immigration of 100,000 Jews to get them out of the degrading refugee camps of war-torn Europe.

President Truman, who had himself been annoyed by the constant pro-Jewish pressure upon him, was even more annoyed with the accusations attributed to Bevin charging Truman with the politics of expediency to get the New York Jewish vote and, even worse, to have the European Jews sent to Palestine to keep them out of the United States.

The result was that Bevin became extremely anti-Jewish. This escalated British-Jewish antagonism in Palestine so that by early 1947 Bevin was determined "to teach the Jews a lesson." It also resulted in the abandonment of Weizmann's leadership by the Zionist movement. Zionism now switched to the hard-line leadership of David Ben-Gurion; the switch was symbolized by the action of the Twenty-Second Congress of the World Zionist Organization meeting in Basel, Switzerland, December 9, 1946, in which Weizmann failed to get approval of his resolution to meet again with the British in the London conference on Palestine, and he failed to be re-elected President of the WZO.

The "bulldog tenacity" of Bevin's powerful and combative personality, which made him very attractive as a Foreign Secretary in "standing up to the Russians" in the rising cold war, was the same quality (in the opinion of many) which made him counterproductive to British interests in Palestine. This school of thought feels that a more pragmatic Bevin, accepting, for instance, the immigration of 100,000 Jews from the refugee camps of Europe, would have defused the international pressures on Britain to the point where the London government could have accommodated the conflict more in line with British interests in the Middle East.

In any case, the Palestine issue escalated out of Bevin's control; Britain decided to abandon Palestine by turning the matter over to the UN and unilaterally withdrawing its presence.

Ernest Bevin died (April 14, 1951) of a heart attack shortly after his seventieth birthday. He had just recently agreed to step down as Foreign Secretary for a less demanding job in the Labor government.

It was a rather sobering situation for Ernest Bevin when the new Labor Foreign Secretary took over the responsibility of planning the post-war international reconstruction policy of a great power hopelessly sliding into a second-rate status. Very quickly he began to see that the reality of the situation required a pro-Arab position as far as British national interests were concerned. When, for instance, the Arab-Jewish violence in Palestine escalated in 1948, the Soviet Union's charges that the British were arming and encouraging the Arab armies to take action against the Jews in Palestine were at least partially true. "Bevin repeatedly encouraged King Abdullah of Jordan to send his British officered Arab Legion into Palestine as the Mandate expired."[2]

Britain's Economic Weakness

Other constraints became increasingly obvious to the London government; British commitments to the Middle East would have to be scaled down to what could financially be supported. As outlined by Bevin, (1) the military presence necessary to protect the Suez Canal, the flow of Persian Gulf oil, and land and air routes to the East would have to be scaled down to a few viable bases instituted *with consent* by the governments in whose territory they were located. Furthermore, (2) getting voluntary consent would probably be a function of the British government's success in finding a solution to the Palestine problem *acceptable to the Arabs*.

In this perspective, the problem Secretary Bevin faced was, of course, the Zionist opposition in Palestine. Bevin, in bargaining with the Arabs for these "voluntary consent" bases, sought to utilize the rigorous enforcement of the 1939 White Paper in terms of the prohibition both (1) of Jewish immigration to Palestine and (2) of the Jewish purchase of Arab land there. However, Arab nationalists were not impressed with Bevin's dilemma, and these pro-Arab efforts by the British Foreign Secretary did not win support nor overcome, in general, the Arabs' sensitivity to colonialism.

In the almost two years between March of 1946 and January of 1948, the British attempted to renegotiate treaties with their Arab client states in the Middle East only to fail everywhere except in Jordan—a national community so limited in viability that the British efforts could hardly be considered successful. In January, 1948, the Portsmouth Treaty with Iraq failed to be ratified. Similarly, the negotiated treaty with Egypt (the Sidqi-Bevin initialed agreement of October, 1946) had met the same fate earlier.

Britain Seeks Other "Consent Bases"

With the Russians still occupying northern Persia, it was the Imperial Staff which had presented the urgency of these "consent bases" to the British Foreign Office in early 1946. In May the British Chiefs of Staff finally were persuaded to acquiesce in a proposed offer to evacuate Egypt on the condition that adequate "consent" military bases would be secured elsewhere. The requirements set up by the Chiefs of Staff for these bases included not only barracks and landing rights but also (1) storage and repair facilities, (2) ample water supplies, (3) adequate local labor supplies, and (4) a good port.

Proposed military bases as alternatives to Egypt were (1) Palestine as a whole including inland air and ground facilities, plus Haifa as a naval base with adequate oil facilities— coupled with a heavy equipment storage area at McKinnon Road, a railway siding in Kenya, and (2) Libya. Cyprus was also suggested but the British army considered it inadequate.

Britain Decides to Quit Palestine

The decision in favor of Palestine for a military base set in motion the enormous task of moving the vast military supplies of the Egyptian bases to Palestine and Kenya. The process of transferring supplies from Egypt to Palestine was, however, very suddenly terminated when, at the United Nations, the British government announced on September 26, 1947, its decision to quit Palestine. Of note is the fact that the Soviets were at least realistic in their concern about entrenched British interests in Palestine and, consequently, the belief that the UN partition plan, with its evacuation of the British presence, might become stalled.

It should be noted that the Jewish leaders also tried bargaining with the British and were not unwilling to bring in the issue of the "consent bases." In a private meeting (shortly before the opening of the second stage of the London Conference in early 1947) between Foreign Secretary Bevin and Ben Gurion, the latter bluntly asked Bevin whether he was holding out against the Jews because of these bases.

Ben Gurion then went on to indicate the possible willingness of the Jews to accept a British naval lease at Haifa and military bases in the Negev region if and when these base areas would become a part of the Jewish state in Palestine. To this bait, the British Foreign Secretary seemed to react with considerable interest.[3] Later, Bevin abandoned the idea.

In the end, Jewish terrorist activity in Palestine, plus irresistible pro-Jewish pressure from the United States, combined to create a cost factor which the British could not accept for long. This the Soviets realized, and, by utilizing the tactic of supporting the Zionists' objective of partition, the Soviet Union ultimately attained its objective of getting the British out of Palestine. Once this was accomplished, it could reverse the field, similarly, and cash in on the subsequent Western dilemma; it could seriously weaken the Western containment policy of the 1950s by a pro-Arab stance—not to mention getting the Western powers out of the other Arab states by the same policy in support of Arab nationalism.

NOTES

1. Howard M. Sachar, *Europe Leaves the Middle East, 1936–1954* (New York: Alfred A. Knopf, 1972), p. 434.

2. Arnold Krammer, *The Forgotten Friendship* (Urbana, Ill.: University of Illinois Press, 1974), p. 23.

3. Barnet Litvinoff, *Ben-Gurion of Israel* (London: Oxford University Press, 1954), p. 173.

CHAPTER 2:

Early Soviet Orientation Toward Jews and Zionism

Historically, Russia's policy toward the Middle East could be described as renewed overt efforts—during the reigns of Peter I and Catherine the Great—at territorial expansion against the Ottoman Empire. In the nineteenth century, under conditions of rapidly fading Ottoman power, it became popular to refer to the situation as the "Eastern Question," and it involved intense rivalry between Austria and Russia for filling in the political vacuum resulting from the increasing decadence of the Sultan's government. Russia pursued its objectives not only via conventional diplomatic and military means, but also by using the ideological media of the Russian Orthodox Church and the Pan-Slavic movement.

Russian Treatment of Jews

Russia, like other countries, has a record of private acts as well as government initiated or permitted acts against the Jews. The human trait of enhancing one's own group identity by discriminating or denigrating other cultural groups was not, of course, limited to Jews. Yet of all the minorities, the Jews of Russia received an extra measure of discrimination. "The Tsars were convinced that the pious, orthodox Russian peasants needed to be protected from an exploitation of alien infidels—the Jews."[1] There was no separation of church and state in Russia.

19

During the nineteenth century Western Europe prided it-self on its liberal progress—with the Jews officially gaining the rights and duties of full citizenship, and beginning to play leading roles in government, business, music, science, law, etc. Even so, this increasing prominence created increased animosity because the Jew now began to compete successfully with the gentile elite. "Dangerous jealousies—even hatreds—were aroused by increasing Jewish prominence and success. With their outstanding qualities, and the traditions of ethnic solidarity and mutual help bred by centuries of oppression, this success was inevitable in all those countries where they now enjoyed the full protection of the laws and a share in the public life."[2] The hatred was only increased when some Jews such as Karl Marx, Leon Trotsky, etc. were found in revolutionary movements.

Directly relevant to this experience in the West was the Russian situation at the time of the assassination of Tsar Alexander II by the Russian revolutionaries in early 1881. The successor regime of Alexander III reacted quickly toward the leftists (which included liberal Jews of metropolitan areas such as St. Petersburg) who were charged with responsibility for the bomb. New outbursts of *pogroms* (massacres) and discriminatory regulations against the Jews followed.

Jews Respond to Persecution

Fear and despair returned to the Jewish communities of Russia. Emigration became the new aspiration of the day. Lovers of Zion (Hoverei Zion), a Jewish organization dedicated to organizing immigration to Palestine, was created in 1884. Representatives of Hoverei Zion played a major role at the organizational conference of the World Zionist Organization at Basel, Switzerland, in 1897.

Zionism was illegal in Russia, yet by the eve of World War I approximately forty Jewish settlements had been established in Palestine. These activities should be seen in the context of

European-wide Jewish thought stimulated by the periodic re-
newal of hostilities against them. Persecuted Jewish communities in the century before World War I underwent a
pointed re-appraisal of their identity in terms of the classical
alternatives of (1) assimilation, (2) leftist internationalism, (3)
flight to a safer environments (to the more individual and
human rights oriented governments of Western civilization),
or (4) Zionism.

While many European Jews immigrated to Palestine, many
more (perhaps 500,000) left for the United States. The new
discriminatory laws against Jews after 1881, supported by increasingly large pogroms, tended to eliminate assimilation as a
viable alternative in Tsarist Russia. For those who remained,
two competing movements sought to enlist the support of the
Jews. One was the revolutionary Jewish workers' organization
known as the Bund, the supporters of which had chosen "leftist internationalism" as the solution to their persecution and
their identity crisis. They bitterly denounced members of the
rival solution to the problem, the Zionists, who were accused
of "chickening out" on the inevitable class struggle by holding
to the utopian opportunism of reactionary nationalism. The
Zionists, in turn, accused the Bund members of shirking their
duty as Jews to help in the national emancipation of their
persecuted brethren. The clandestine Communist organization in Russia was distinct from the Jewish Bund but sided
with the latter in ideological confrontation with the Zionists.
The British promise of a "national home" for Jews in the Balfour Declaration of World War I only increased the antagonism against Zionists in that the latter were now charged
with collusion with big-power capitalist imperialism.

Communism's Opposition to Zionism

Even before Communism could claim power in a single
state, its leaders charged Zionism with the decadent and reac-

tionary aspirations not only of being interested in (1) nationalism instead of supporting the international class struggle, but also in (2) the self-deception of religion as the "opiate of the people." The Communists criticized the Zionists' aspirations to use religion as the foundation for a new state instead of the Marxist truth of economic production and class conflict as the prime movers in human society. In 1913 Stalin criticized Zionism as a "reactionary and nationalist movement recruiting its followers from among the Jewish petty and middle bourgeoisie of the Jewish workers." This proposed Jewish state in Palestine would effectively eliminate the Jewish proletariat "from the general struggle of the proletariat."[3]

The February, 1917, revolution legalized Zionism, sparking a burst of renewed Zionist activity. This created problems for the Bolshevik revolutionaries who seized power in October of the same year. No strong measures against Jewish organizations were taken immediately; all energies had to be devoted to survival. The original tolerance of Zionism was publicly rationalized by acknowledging that the organizations' cultural and educational activity was not in conflict with official Communist programs. There were a number of Jews in the leadership elite of the Communist party. In fact, the new government included a Jewish section, the Commissariat for Jewish Affairs, organizationally under the supervision of the People's Commissariat for Nationality Affairs. The major responsibility of the former was working with the Jewish Communist movement. Considerable Jewish support and participation was achieved by a series of "Palestine Weeks" held in different Russian cities.[4]

Outside of the Jewish Communist movement, Jewish cultural traditions were tolerated unless they began to seriously contradict the party line. No rival ideology (religion) could be tolerated by the party. The formal religious practices of the Jews were circumscribed similarly to those of the Orthodox and other Christian groups.

The Soviet's First Priority: Survival

After the Communist revolution in 1917, Moscow's expansion to the south emphasized ideological conversion instead of increased territorial claims. The First Congress of the Third International met in 1919. It was essentially an emergency meeting dedicated to the task of survival in the face of challenges from the White Russian armies with foreign support. The First Congress of the "Toilers of the East" convened at Baku in September, 1920. By this time the military challenge had been met, and it addressed itself to the peoples of the Muslim world. It sought Muslim support against the European presence in the Middle East border lands. Officially adopted at the Baku conference was a statement on liberating the peoples of the Middle East. Firstly, the *external yoke* of colonialism would have to be removed. Once this was accomplished, the second requirement was to remove the *internal yoke* of exploitation by feudal landlords and the capitalist class; the challenge involved a two-step sequence: (1) national independence and then (2) the elimination of class exploitation from within.[5]

Zionists Condemned in the 1930s

By 1930 Zionism was censured as exploitive imperialism against the Arabs. In an open letter of the Executive Committee of the Comintern, November 20, 1930, it was officially held that:

> Zionism is the exponent of the exploiting, big power, imperialist oppressive strivings of the Hebrew bourgeoisie which uses the oppressed position of the Hebrew minority in eastern Europe for imperialist policy and for the securing of their domination. To realize this purpose, Zionism was linked by the mandate and the Balfour Declaration with British imperialism. Zionism

was converted into a weapon of British imperialism in order to suppress the national liberation movement of the Arab masses at the same time that it converted into its own weapon the Hebrew population of Palestine down to the semiproletarian and proletarian layers.[6]

The Soviet Union has also had a latent uneasiness about the possibility of Zionism taking hold among Soviet Jews and creating difficulties for the maintenance of national unity. Not only did the Soviets fear a threat to the integrity of the state from rising Jewish identity, the Kremlin leaders saw danger in Zionism sparking nationalism in other minorities. This was viewed as exposing Soviet national security by creating opportunities for foreign interference via "fifth column" possibilities.

Soviet Condemnation of Turkish Nationalism

Russian expansion at the expense of the Ottoman Empire had brought large numbers of Muslims, including many Turkish communities, inside the effective territorial claims of Russia long before the Soviet Revolution. Particularly after the Young Turk Revolution in 1908, the "Russification" efforts upon these Turkish communities re-invigorated a Pan-Turanian movement in Turkey with the aspirations of a supranational unity of Turkish-speaking peoples.

The Soviets criticized Pan-Turanism as a form of nationalism belonging to the decadent world of capitalist exploitation and imperialism. Pan-Islamism, similarly, was condemned by Stalin in his famous treatise on the national question four years before the successful revolution in Russia.

During World War I the Ottoman invasion of southern Russia in conjunction with a Pan-Muslim and Pan-Turkish ideological offensive had given the Tsarist government some uneasy moments. Also, before Germany's defeat in 1918, the Kaiser's government extended diplomatic recognition to the proclaimed independent state of Azerbaijan, carved out of former Russian territory. Furthermore, again at Russian territorial expense, the Paris Peace Conference moved to create an expanded, independent state of Armenia. The fact that neither of these states ultimately prevailed was little comfort to the Soviets in terms of their concerns about the problem.

The Soviet Union's Muslim Minority

By World War II the Soviet Union had a Muslim minority in its southern territories of perhaps 30 million people, making up about 14 percent of its population. There were attempts at using these minorities of Russia—in this case those oriented toward the Middle East cultures—for "fifth column" purposes. While Operation Barbarossa (code name for the June 22, 1941, German invasion of Russia) seemed to be irresistibly deep inside Russia, the rising tide of Pan-Turanism took hold in Turkey with the behind-the-scenes blessing of certain government officials. The Nazi German government also coordinated an Islamic propaganda appeal in conjunction with its military offensive. To some in these Muslim communities of Russia, the propaganda was strikingly effective. They collaborated with the German armies, and suffered Stalin's wrath in 1944 when he gave orders to liquidate the four autonomous Muslim republics of the Crimea, Balkar, Ingush, and Chechen.

Friendly Treatment of Kurds

The Soviet Union, after it started winning, attempted to utilize the "fifth column" potential of these minority groups to build a *cordon sanitaire* of political entities under its control along its Middle East borders. These efforts included peoples such as the Kurds, Azerbaijanis, Georgians, and Armenians. Mulla Mustafa Barzani and his Kurdish rebel group from Iraq not only received arms from, but spent a number of years in, the Soviet Union. It was, therefore, not unexpected for the Soviet leaders to consider another minority group, the Jews, with similar possibilities.

The Soviets Organize "A Refuge" for the Jews

It is interesting to note that the Soviet Union made several attempts to find a "refuge" for Russian Jews within its own state. In this case the stated motive was to help the Jewish urban population solve its economic difficulties. In the early 1920s the Soviet government sought to organize a Jewish settlement in the Crimea. Plans called for several hundred thousand Jews to be resettled in an agricultural project there. Eventually this Jewish Crimean settlement was to become a Jewish republic of the USSR.[7] However, opposition from the vested interests of the native residents of the Crimea, plus the lack of adequate available agricultural land, terminated the effort.

Biro-Bidjan

On March 28, 1928, a decree of the Presidium of the Central Executive Committee proposed to set aside land for a Jewish colony in the Far Eastern province of Biro-Bidjan. This involved an area of 14,208 square miles along the Amur River adjoining Manchuria. The Soviet government, in October, 1931, proclaimed the settlement a national Jewish administrative unit. In 1934 it was formally proclaimed a Jewish Autonomous Region. The motivation for Soviet policy seems to have been twofold. Primarily, it was an action "aimed at building up Zionist Jewry into a socialist people as an antidote to the Zionist clamour for a National Home in Palestine."[8] Secondly, having noted the Japanese expansionist thrusts in the Far East, Stalin decided to push the region as a Jewish province in an effort to settle the sparsely populated areas and contribute to the territorial integrity and national security of Russia. In 1939 the Jewish Autonomous Region was officially made a part of the Soviet Far Eastern Territory, and Yiddish was proclaimed as the official language.[9] Of particular interest is the fact that in the mid-1930s a small number of Jews— perhaps 600—from Lithuania, Poland, Argentina, and other countries settled there in addition to Soviet Jews. However, the expectations of massive Jewish migration to Biro-Bidjan never materialized. The Yiddish Communist newspaper, the Moscow *Emes*, estimated the Jewish population of Biro-Bidjan to be 29,000 as of 1937.[10] However, the Jewish settlement also felt the impact of Stalin's purges in 1937. For the most part, the crucial leadership of the Jewish region was destroyed by imprisonment, exile, and execution. The beloved Professor Liberberg was quietly arrested and secretly executed.[11] Final destruction of the area's vitality as a Jewish region was achieved by Stalin in 1948 when he not only destroyed the Jewish leadership, as in 1937, but struck a direct blow at Jewish culture by closing down every Jewish school, publishing house, and theater.[12] The purges, the lack of any historical-religious attachment to the area, and the harsh physical environment destroyed Biro-Bidjan as a Jewish national settlement in the USSR.

Anti-Semitism in Poland

Passing reference might also appropriately be made to the 1937 anti-Semitic efforts demonstrated by Poland (and to some degree by Rumania) to get rid of Jews by exiling them to Madagascar. This plan was actually pushed by the Polish government; a mission was sent to Madagascar to implement the proposal. The ultimate failure of the project was due in large part to the strong opposition which it created among the people of the island itself.

Hitler proposed a similar project to sweep out the Jews in 1940–41. This effort was again stillborn; he decided, alternatively, on the "final solution" of extermination in the death camps.

None of the Western democracies was willing to make a significant exception in their immigration policy to accommodate the Jews who were bearing the brunt of German persecution. President Roosevelt took the initiative in calling for an international conference to deal with the problem. In response, the Evian Inter-governmental Conference on Refugees was convened in 1938. Nothing of significance was achieved.

Western Proposals for a Jewish "Home"

There were approximately a dozen serious proposals for Jewish colonization presented as solutions to the Jews fleeing persecution—particularly in Germany—in the 1930s. The British made suggestions such as British Guiana, Kenya, Uganda, Northern Rhodesia, and Tanganyika. Even the United States got into the act when Secretary of the Interior, Harold Ickes, proposed a plan for Jewish settlement in Alaska.

Other proposals included Cyrenaica, Ecuador, Brazil, Angola, northwestern Australia, etc. A Dominican Republic invitation for the Jewish refugees—the so-called Sosua Settlement—actually did get underway. President Trujillo offered to absorb 100,000 refugees on his huge Sosua estate. Some Jewish refugees did accept the offer, but it was only a very small percentage of the original projection (presumably only 413 ever arrived in conjunction with Trujillo's proposal).[13]

After these abortive efforts, one would have expected statesmen to anticipate great difficulties with Zionists' demands in the post-war period. These, of course, did occur, and it was the Soviet Union which utilized the Jewish attraction to Palestine, in the face of frustrated Arab nationalism, to further its national interests in the process of re-creating the post-war public order.

NOTES

1. Surendra Bhutani, *Israeli Soviet Cold War* (Delhi, India: Atul Prakashan, 1975), p. 2.

2. Richard Allen, *Imperialism and Nationalism in the Fertile Crescent* (London: Oxford University Press, 1974), p. 191.

3. Joseph V. Stalin, "Marxism and the National Question," *Collected Works* (Moscow, 1952), vol. 2, p. 335.

4. *The Zionist Review,* vol. 2, no. 3 (July, 1918), p. 34.

5. U. S., Congress, House, Committee on Foreign Affairs, *Communism in the Near East* (1948), p. 23.

6. Bhutani, p. 7.

7. *Palestine Affairs,* March, 1946.

8. Ibid.

9. Ibid.

10. Ben Ami, *Between Hammer and Sickle* (Philadelphia: The Jewish Publication Society of America, 1967), p. 238.

11. Ibid.

12. *Palestine Affairs,* March, 1946.

CHAPTER 3:

Pre-1947 Soviet Contacts with Palestine Communists and Zionists

After World War I a modest "third immigration wave" of some 30,000 Jews from eastern Europe came to Palestine. The lot of the peasant and petty bourgeoisie groups in eastern Europe was rather difficult in the seething post-World War I turbulence characterized by civil strife, revolution, and the violent reactionary efforts of the pre-war elites. Yet even under these post-war conditions, the Zionist idea attracted only a limited number of Jews to Palestine. Most of the young, politically conscious Jews (like their Polish, Hungarian, or Russian gentile counterparts) found their challenge in nationalist and social liberation movements in the land of their birth.

Ideological Conflict

However, among those that did experience the call to Palestine, contradictory ideological considerations were common. The attraction of Zionism is well documented. Alternatively—and at least to some degree contradictorily— the newer, more secularized ideologies of liberalism, nationalism, and revolutionism sometimes overshadowed Zionism which, for these people, had its roots in what the Jewish young people sometimes experienced as ossified, archaic orthodoxy of the Jewish religious traditions.

The Communist Party in Palestine

The beginning of modern Communist organizations in Palestine dates back to 1919, although admission to the Comintern did not come until 1924. After World War I, Communism seemed for a time to be the rising star of political movements and party organizations. Communist governments were at one time set up in Bavaria and Hungary as well as, of course, in Russia. The Communist party's experience in Palestine in the inter-war years is perhaps unmatched in terms of confusion, conflict, and contradictions. In fact, the Communist party of Palestine—although always a very small group relative to those whose primary identity was Zionism—time and time again broke up into disarray over conflicting and irreconcilable positions.

Zionism Versus Communism

To the Jewish Communists, Zionism was officially a reactionary-imperialistic movement which erred in its failure to understand the true challenge of class identity and social revolution. The act of immigrating to Palestine for Zionist purposes was contradictory to the official Communist line which they came to hold.

Early in the experience of the Palestine Communist movement an attempt was made to reconcile the conflict by supporting Jewish settlements with an identity, not in Zionism, but in the peasant and worker classes—a movement purged of Zionism. Thus, for those immigrants in the Communist movement of Palestine who had cultural roots in Judaism, this conflict should be seen in terms of the previously mentioned alternatives of the Jewish identity crisis: (1) Zionism, versus (2) "leftist internationalism," i.e., Communism.

With an identity in Communism, the urgent task was to eliminate the images of *imperialism* and the *nationalism* of Zionism (obviously a contradiction). Some immigrant Jewish

Communists felt it necessary to take a pro-Arab, anti-Jewish stance. This tended to be another self-defeating position because Arabs generally refused to join the Communist organization, and the party could hardly expect great success in converts from Jewish groups which it felt compelled to condemn.

Leftist Jewish immigrants found it quite impossible to consider the frequent Arab violence against them as being *progressive* (as Marxists use the term). Yet the situation became even more contradictory when they were forced to rely on British protection from Arab violence, since they were strongly opposed to British imperialism. "Marxist Zionists," to use Walter Laqueur's term, "continued to claim . . . that the Jewish national movement had nothing in common with imperialism." They identified it as a "working class," "proletariat" movement which would overcome current Arab-Jewish antagonism.

> The Arab revolt, according to this interpretation, was provoked both by the British policy of divide and rule and by the clerico-fascist Arab exploiters who feared Jewish working-class immigration because it heralded social and economic change. The spokesmen of the Zionist left proclaimed that the Jewish revolutionary working-class movement was the only fortress of progress and Socialism in the Middle East, and promised that with its help a strong Arab proletarian movement would emerge, leading eventually to a Jewish-Arab workers' state in Palestine.[1]

Alternatively, the Palestine Communist Party viewed the situation in a different light. Shortly before the 1936 rebellion the party executive decided that the "Arab Communists should actively participate in destroying Zionism and imperialism while the Jewish members should do their share by weakening the Yishuv [Jewish community] from within."[2]

The Seventh Congress of the Comintern debated the Arab-Jewish situation in Palestine. One rather important voice of the congress, A. Liebling, proclaimed that " 'our task is to show the Jewish workers that their national and class interests are connected with the victory of the Arab liberation movement.' "[3] But the Communist voices were far from united. Another Congress participant, even less sympathetic to the Jews, proclaimed that " 'the Jewish minority in Palestine is a colonizing minority by its very nature.' "[4]

Palestine Communists and Their Relation to Moscow

Usually, Communist party leaders in Palestine accepted the official party line handed down from Moscow. Emphasis upon the sanctity of the official dogma is a well-known characteristic of the Communist political order. Communist parties in Palestine, like Communist parties anywhere, were of necessity concerned about their authenticity. As a major anchor of belief in a system which sanctifies dogma, there could only be one road to truth—a situation which explains why national Communist parties, even into the decade of the 1970s, devoted so much energy and emotion to the determination of leadership in the periodic international Communist party conferences. Thus, the Palestine Communist organization, like those in most states, found itself compelled to recognize the Soviet Communist party as its 'Pope" to which it belonged and to whose final determination of doctrine it must conform. However, for a variety of reasons the Soviets never effectively exploited the Comintern ties to Palestine.

Expelled from the Comintern

In 1937 the party was expelled from the Comintern; by 1938 the Communist movement in Palestine was splintered and without a significant membership.[5] It had led a volatile existence in the thirteen years since it joined the Comintern in 1924.[6]

The Soviet Union had other possibilities besides the Palestine Communist Party to promote its influence—note, for instance, the possibilities in the general nationalist ferment and political instability of the turbulent Palestine Mandate. Given the constraints of national decision-making in the Kremlin, these opportunities were never fully developed.

The Communist Party Divided

Let us return to the life of Communist organizations in Palestine. It represents an era of major significance in understanding Soviet relations with Israel in its first decade. As suggested previously, the disintegration of the Communist party was due primarily to the tension arising between (1) those who accepted the legitimacy of Jewish immigration to Palestine and basic equality of Jew and Arab as long as the former was sufficiently "de-Zionized" and (2) those who accepted the Soviet line of opposition to Jewish immigration, who insisted on Arab predominance in the Palestine Communist Party leadership,and who emphasized a revolutionary attitude on the class struggle (in contrast to liberal, evolutionary approaches to social improvement). The anti-Jewish Communist party leaders had trouble keeping the above pro-Jewish faction in the fold. When pushed too hard, these groups would join the leftwing groups of the Jewish labor party. These Communists took part in the creation of the Histadrut (the General Federation of Jewish Labour).

In the first election (December, 1920) they won seven out of the Histadrut's eighty-seven seats.[7] This "rightist," pro-Jewish wing of the Communist party (the so-called M.O.P.S.[8]), lasted less than a year. Its demise resulted from being squeezed out of viability by the power of forces on both its political right and left. The M.O.P.S. group did not reject Zionism completely; although it criticized Zionists for supporting creative or evolutionary change in social progress rather than the proper "proletarian Zionism" emphasizing revolution and class struggle.[9] The group was also to the "right" of the main stream of Communist thinking because it opposed membership in the Third International.

M.O.P.S. came to the end of its short existence as a result of the May Day riots of 1921 when the British Mandatory authorities arrested and deported its leaders, having charged the organization with responsibility for the death of a number of Jews resulting from a clash of rival demonstrations in Jaffa between M.O.P.S. and the Jewish Trade Union groups.

The Afula Swamp Clash

As the years passed, the mainstream of Palestine Communists moved more decisively under Moscow's policy directives—a policy which became more anti-Zionist and more pro-Arab.

Violence repeatedly marked the inter-war period of the Palestine Mandate. For example, there was the 1924 "Afula Case" in which Arab beduin and fellaheen attacked the New Zionists settlers of the Afula swamp. The Communist party now overtly condemned the newly-organized Jewish settlement there through its slogan of "revolutionary action" which was used to incite the Arabs against the Afula Jewish settlers. The Communists condemned the injustice of the Zionist imperialists who were colonizing the Jezreel Valley at the expense of the rightful Arab owners.

The blood-letting was finally stopped by reinforced police intervention. The Jews charged the Communists as primarily responsible for the violence against its community.[10]

The 1929 Riots

More serious were the 1929 riots which began by a Jewish-Muslim (Arab) clash at the Wailing Wall. The Arabs killed 133 Jews[11] and seriously injured more than twice that number. Jewish retaliation was minimal at this time.

The experience of the Palestine Communist party in these riots is, while tragic, most interesting to recall. By this time, Moscow had succeeded in establishing a controlling influence over the local Communist party; although there were some short-run exceptions—particularly those associated with internal party strife. Nevertheless, in 1929 before the August riots began, the Sixth Congress of the Comintern had changed its policy by condemning the previous accommodation with the various native nationalist organizations. The newly adopted line now condemned the traitorous *bourgeois* parties of the East such as the Wafd party of Egypt, the Kuomintang of China, Attasi's organization in Syria, etc. These groups were now categorized as unacceptably *reformist* instead of latently *revolutionary,* which required that they be condemned instead of supported.

Moscow Criticizes the Palestine Communists

The Palestine Communists had just taken this Moscow-determined policy line when the Arab-Jewish confrontation exploded in mid-August. The violence of the events undeniably gave the situation a revolutionary or "revolting" characteristic, but one which did *not* conform to Communist perceptions of reality. The violence broke out over the clash of Arab and Jewish (Zionist) nationalists, not between the exploited and the exploiters or imperialists (the British). The Palestine Communist line was officially that of supporting a common Arab-Jewish front against the British exploiters—colonial uprisings against the imperialists. But the violence between Jews and Arabs tended to leave the Communists in a state of confusion and inaction. The net result was that the official Moscow line, with its momentary indecision, left the Palestine Communists out of the vanguard of "revolutionary struggle" where their ideology dictated their proper role to be. They had "missed the boat."

Purge of the Communist Party

This missed opportunity was sharply criticized in the new instructions received from Moscow in September. The new directive required a 180 degree "about-face" and a purge of the party. Moscow now dictated a new policy of supporting the Arab revolt by making sure the Palestine Communists would be in the vanguard of violence in the next overt confrontation. No more should a reactionary like the Grand Mufti of Jerusalem be allowed to brush aside the Palestine Comintern affiliates and lead the violent revolutionary upheavals in the British "colony" of Palestine.[12]

In reassessing its errors, the party concluded that it had failed in establishing support and leadership of the Arab masses who were a people of revolutionary potential—a people awaiting the leadership which the Communists were "destined to give." The word from Moscow was that all party members who could not support the definitive pro-Arab thrust of policy must be purged from the party. By this purging, the Palestine Communist party obviously antagonized the Jewish communities. As a result, the Jewish communities initiated active opposition to the Palestine Communist party. Needless to say, this action was a severe blow to the party, for leftist or Communist ideology had originally been more appealing to Jewish liberals than to the Arabs.

Communist Failure: Recruitment

The deterioration in the Palestine Communist party's effectiveness was also the result of its inability to win support from the Arabs, whose cause they were supporting at the cost of alienating the Jews. The Arab proletariat of the cities (such as it was) did not respond to Communist ideology, and the rural Arabs (fellaheen) found their identity in the Muslim leadership focused on the person of the Grand Mufti of Jerusalem. Finally, the inability of the Communist party to become a significant force in Palestine politics of the Mandate period was also due to the great inter-Arab rivalries between Nashashibis and Husseinis. The Nashashibi family, although usually controlling the mayoralty of Jerusalem, was very sensitive to its generally inferior political situation in relation to the Husseini family with its powerful hold on the Muslim religious structure of Palestine. In fact, some of the sophisticated, middle-class Nashashibis were open to an alliance of forces with the Jews to counterbalance the power represented by Hejj Amin el Husseini.[13] In the 1936–37 Arab general strike and political upheaval against the British, the Nashashibi-Husseini antagonism exploded into frequent cases of violence and assassinations between the Arab groups. This further complicated the efforts of the weak Palestine Communist group which now saw Jews as their primary enemy.

Clash of Soviet Interests: National Versus Ideological

There was, however, also some equivocation in Soviet support for the Arabs against Zionism in the inter-war period. This dimension of Soviet policy toward the Jews was another Middle East case of the inherent contradiction in Soviet policy between (1) Russia's concern for its national interests— playing the accepted rules of "the international establishment"—and (2) the subversive game of clandestine support for the (usually outlawed) foreign Communist parties. For example, there was a Soviet re-appraisal of its pro-Arab ideology in the face of increasing Arab attraction to German and Italian fascism in the latter 1930s. But to complicate matters even more, important Arab national leaders also sensed a danger of Italian and German aggression against the Middle East. This impact was to some degree responsible for Egypt's willingness to come to terms with Britain in the Anglo-Egyptian Treaty of 1936. With these Arab leaders drawing closer to the "capitalist–imperialist" British and French in the Middle East, the Soviet support for the Arab nationalists in opposition to the Zionists also cooled.

Soviet Policy Reversals

An even more radical swing of the Soviet Middle East foreign policy line occurred in conjunction with the German-Soviet non-aggression treaty of August, 1939. As a result of this

shift of Russian policy, Moscow, for instance, supported the
pro-Axis coup attempted by Rashid Ali in Iraq in spring, 1941.
The small Communist parties in Palestine found it difficult
(and embarrassing, to say the least) to switch their policy lines
to conform with these wide gyrations of Moscow's policy.

With Hitler now the alliance partner of the Socialist fatherland, the Palestine Communist party found it necessary again
to dove-tail and turn the proverbial 180 degrees. This was
rationalized, interestingly enough, by proclaiming that Hitler's character had changed; he had become the obedient servant of Moscow and was no longer the partner in imperialist
collusion with Chamberlain and Daladier.[14] The new focus of
public statements was on condemning the Western powers of
Britain and France as warmongers.

After the tenuous Russo-German friendship treaty of August, 1939 was torn asunder by the overwhelming military
strike of "Operation Barbarossa" on June 22, 1941, both of the
two major Communist groups[15] found it quite impossible to
make another immediate policy reversal, as called for by the
German attack on Russia. For four months the earlier position
of exhortation against Palestinians enlisting in the imperialist
British army was continued. The June onslaught against
Soviet Russia was conceptualized as collusion of Britain and
(free) France with the fascists against Russia.

Grand Mufti Denounced as Fascist

Nevertheless, the Soviet Union's pressure upon the Palestinian Communists continued; they were pressured to conform to the dazzling vacillation of Soviet fortunes in international life. Moscow now denounced the violently anti-Zionist
Arab leader of Palestine, the Grand Mufti of Jerusalem, Hejj
Amin el Husseini, as a tool of the German and Italian fascists,
and encouraged Arab and Jewish cooperation in Palestine.

Only in October of 1941 did the official Palestine Communist line change to announce its support for a united front

against the Axis; it now reversed its policy and approved the Histadrut's call for Palestine volunteers to join the British army in a common effort against the fascist foes.

Palestine Communists after World War II

At the end of World War II the Communists in Palestine sought to change their radical image to that of a "respectable party" similar to the other main stream political groups in the British-controlled territory. Among the Jewish Communists, the leadership passed to men of less crusading spirit such as Meir Vilner and Ester Vilenska, while the same trend was visible among the Palestinian Arab Communists in such leaders as Emil Habib, Emil Tuma and Tawfiq Tubi.[16]

The Jewish Communists now were still anti-Zionists—condemning the idea of a Jewish state—but less militant about it. They emphasized their attachment to international socialism in general and to the Soviet Union, whose prestige was magnified by its victory over Nazi Germany. The Jewish terrorist organizations were condemned. In 1946 a policy modification was made. While earlier there was a straight condemnation of Zionism, now the objective was the creation of a "democratic" Arab-Jewish state with the Jews filling one-third of the important government positions. The outspoken 1947 UN speech by Gromyko supporting the creation of a Jewish state necessitated another embarrassing reversal of the Communist line in Palestine to dove-tail with the Soviet's new position. As a matter of fact, the Communists originally sought to reduce their loss of face by proclaiming that Gromyko's position in the UN had been misunderstood and erroneously reported. Yet in the end, the party had to "eat crow" and accept the embarrassment.

As if this weren't enough, another flip-flop would be required of the party line. In September, the Communist party (of Palestine) advocated the inclusion of Jerusalem in the Jewish state and condemned the United States' position which advocated the internationalization of the Holy City. Then the Soviets came out with a position in support of internationalization. This forced the Palestine Communist party (MAKI) to dove-tail again with the Soviets, leaving it to the former to rationalize its way out of the contradiction.

But the disastrous vacillations were not yet over. In late spring the Soviets changed positions again and declared *against* the internationalization of Jerusalem. Once more a retraction was called for by MAKI.

In summarizing the Soviet relationship to Palestine Communist parties, and the former's support of the creation of Israel, it is important to remember that the Communists of Palestine were really quite ineffective in gaining new converts and were plagued with endless party strife. Soviet policy could readily disregard the interests of the Communist movements of the Levant if its national interests so dictated. In any case, where interests contradicted ideology, it was always possible to rationalize the policy through a "new interpretation" of Marxist-Leninist thought.

Palestine Jews and Russia during World War II

After June, 1941, opportunities arose for Zionist contacts with the Soviet Union. There was an easing of restrictions on contacts between Soviet subjects and the outside world. With the threat of defeat, the Russian government was open to sympathy and support from any foreign group which might be able to help.

A Jewish anti-fascist organization was among some two dozen such groups founded in Moscow at this time. This Soviet Jewish group appealed to the Jewish community in Palestine for aid—an appeal which met with a warm and immediate response. Now the Soviet government was willing to allow, for instance, Soviet Jews to appeal as Jews for help from other Jewish communities.[17]

"Aid to Russia Week"

With the Soviet Union in a violent struggle for its very survival, Zionists moved to grasp a golden opportunity for developing Russian support for the possible creation of a postwar Jewish state. As early as October, 1941, the Yishuv's Histadrut organized an "Aid to Russia Week," emphasizing the raising of money for medical supplies for the Red Army. This proved to be a very successful effort with £10,000 worth of supplies turned over to Soviet Ambassador Maisky in London. (The Zionists were, of course, also motivated to help the Soviets by the fact that a German victory in World War II would be disastrous for any Jews in areas dominated by Hitler's regime.)

At the same time, "A Public Committee to Help the Soviet Union in Its War Against Fascism" was organized by the Jews in Palestine.[18] Seven months later, in one of the Soviets' darkest hours of the war, the Jews in Palestine (although now also supported by the Communists) organized the "V-League to Help the Soviet Union," with numerous branches in the various Jewish settlements.

The V-League

The purpose of the V-League was to provide funds, consumer goods, and medical supplies for Soviet Russia. It was unable to get permission for an office in Moscow, but was successful in establishing one in Teheran which facilitated the channeling of aid to Russia. Needless to say, the League contributed to the rapprochement between the Zionists of Palestine and the Soviet Union, which was later of vital importance in view of the narrow margin by which the UN acted to finally support the creation of Israel. A V-League delegation arrived with a gift of three ambulances, field operating rooms, and other medical supplies which were turned over to Soviet officials in Teheran in April, 1943—"a gift of the Palestine Jews to the Red Army."[19] In a rather moving ceremony accepting these Jewish contributions, the Soviet official expressed the gratitude of his country and suggested that a new era of friendship had begun.

Two more delegations of the V-League (December, 1943, and November, 1944) were sent to Teheran with supplies. Again, an official Soviet government reception was held in Teheran for the November delegation. At the ceremony the Soviet representative said:

> The help given us by the Jewish organization of Palestine is particularly touching. No one knows as well as the peoples of the Soviet Union the suffering and torment caused this people [the Jews] by Fascism, the enemy of mankind. We know how earnestly the Jewish people desire the destruction of this medieval ideology, and therefore how sincere is its help to the Red Army.
>
> One burst of fire in an average section of the front consumes ten carloads of metal. For a single front to operate properly, it needs thousands of carloads of supplies, equipment, fuel, etc. in a single day but we know that these gifts embody not metal alone but also the stuff of Jewish hearts.[20]

Earlier, in late August, 1942, the first national convention of the V-League was held. Two Soviet representatives, Michailov and Petrenko, from the Russian Embassy in Ankara were there as guests of the League.[21] It proved to be another "friendship building" success for the Jews; although the two also met with at least one anti-fascist Arab group. Petrenko and Michailov were guests of the Palestine Jews at a number of Jewish settlements and "were deeply impressed by their meetings with various Jewish groups."[22] *The Zionist Review* reported that the Soviet diplomats were received at one of the original Jewish settlements with the singing, in Hebrew, of "The Internationale" in their honor.[23]

The Zionist Review commented upon the dimension of cultural affinity between the Zionists of Palestine and the Russian Soviets. The paper editorialized thus:

> There are still many people in the Yishuv for whom the love of the Russian people and its literature is part of their cultural herit-

age. After all, a great number of Zionist leaders were born in Russia . . . and Russian Zionists had a tremendous influence on the development of the movement. . . . A number of Histadrut leaders were influenced in their youth by the Russian Revolutionary Movement and found inspiration in the works of the great Russian thinkers, writers, and poets. The builders of communal settlements in Palestine feel deep sympathy with the social ideas which have played such a great part in Russian history for the last 60–70 years.[24]

At the V-League convention in Jerusalem, S. S. Michailov made very complimentary remarks about the friendship with the Jewish people of Palestine:

The help Palestine Jews offered to the peoples of the U.S.S.R., who are fighting the Fascist enemy, will strengthen the ties of friendship between Jewish Palestine and the peoples of the Soviet Union. We appreciate your help, for which you have created the V-League, and we will not forget it.[25]

Expansion of Jewish-Soviet Friendship

By October, 1943, the former Ambassador to London, Ivan Maisky, had been appointed Soviet Deputy Foreign Minister. Later, he paid a visit to Jerusalem and made a special request to see some Jewish settlements.[26] Representatives of the Jewish Agency and the Histadrut—which included David Ben Gurion and Golda Myerson (Meir)—were happy to oblige. Some additional time was devoted to visiting the Jewish quarters in Jerusalem and discussing the difficulties that the British White Paper of 1939 created for the Jewish Agency's interpretation of the Balfour Declaration. More specifically, the discussion focused on that document's promise to the Jews of a "national home" in Palestine.

The visit appears to have been quite successful from the Zionist perspective. Golda Myerson is quoted as having summarized the success as follows:

It was obvious . . . that his [Maisky's] visit was no mere courtesy visit to the Jewish Agency after his meetings in London with

David Ben Gurion, M. Shertok and B. Locker, but that he really
wanted to know whether it was possible to do something in this
country, so that when the time came, when they would have to
express an opinion on the Jewish problem and on Palestine, he
would have first-hand knowledge. We had the feeling that this
visit was of great value.[27]

Bartley Crum and the Anglo-American Committee of Inquiry

Golda Myerson's evaluation was confirmed by the Russians, according to Bartley Crum—an attorney who had just
been appointed by President Truman to serve as one of the six
American members of the Anglo-American Committee of Inquiry on Palestine. Mr. Crum had previously met the Soviet
statesman, Dimitri Manuilsky, at the United Nations San
Francisco conference. The Anglo-American Committee was
holding some hearings in London on the way to Palestine, and
Bartley Crum decided to take the initiative to call on the
former Soviet head of the Comintern (and close associate of
Lenin) at the Soviet Embassy. In the course of the meeting,
Mr. Crum related the following summary of the conversation:

> We went on to talk about the Soviet Union's position on Pales-
> tine. Manuilsky was most careful in his choice of words. Ivan
> Maisky, former Soviet Ambassador to London, he said, visited
> Palestine in 1945, and wrote a glowing report to the Kremlin
> about the magnificent progress the Jews had achieved in Pales-
> tine. He, Manuilsky, in his own city of Kiev, had seen the suffer-
> ings of the Jews, he told me. He knew what they had gone
> through. He was proud that anti-Semitism was not tolerated in
> Russia. But he would be less than honest, he added, if he did not
> tell me also that there is a large Mohammedan population in the
> Soviet Union. . . .
>
> Then he added, "Great Britain, because of her activities in the
> Middle East, may make it impossible for us to accept the recom-

mendations of your committee. She is using the Middle East as the military base of her operations. I believe that she will take her troops out of Egypt into Palestine, and then Palestine and Trans-Jordan will become Britain's arsenal in the Middle East."

He would do all in his power, he said, to help both in relation to Palestine and in opening the doors of the Soviet Union to such Jews as might want to find refuge and rehabilitation there.[28]

Stalin's Historical Opposition to Zionism

In spite of these rather favorable expressions of support by Soviet diplomats, Stalin's historical opposition to Zionism would not be easily set aside—unless, perhaps, other more important Soviet interests might be achieved. To Stalin the Jews could never be considered a nation, and therefore they were not entitled to national self-determination—to say nothing of the more relevant thesis that nationalism was part of the decadent capitalist structure which must give way to the more vital reality of class conflict—a conflict to be transformed into the classless society.

In Stalin's view, the Jews failed to qualify as a nation because they were not a single community united in historical development and having a common language, territory, culture, and economic life. He pointed out that there was quite a gap between the wealthy, sophisticated urban American Jew and the village Jew of the Georgian Soviet Socialist Republic. Nevertheless, Stalin's statements about Jews and their lack of nationality were, to an important degree, rationalizations for the Soviet objectives of domestic tranquility and ideological integrity.

Soviets Hint at Support for Jews

In the Bartley Crum–Dimitri Manuilsky conversation in London's Soviet Embassy, the latter related to Crum how, in spite of the traditional historical difficulty Russia had had with pogroms and Zionism, there was now some new hope. According to Aharon Cohen, Malenkov had expressed a similar empathy for Zionism in the Communist party discussions in Moscow, November, 1944. Malenkov noted the increasing chasm between British policy in Palestine and what the Jews indicated they would accept after the war. The Soviet official pointed out the progressive nature of the Jewish communities in Palestine, and contrasted this with the growing collusion between the reactionary Arab leaders and the British administration of the League of Nations Mandate. The British were cleverly manipulating the peoples of the Middle East to further their hold on the area. Malenkov's position in the Moscow party meeting was one of expressed sympathy for the Jewish suffering in the holocaust of Europe. He felt the Jews should stand up to the British in Palestine. Representatives of the Yishuv received reports of the Soviet discussions with a great deal of satisfaction and hope. Perhaps the Soviet Union might support their rights to a homeland in Palestine after the war.[29]

Even before the end of World War II there was further evidence of Soviet sympathetic consideration for the Jews in Palestine. In 1944, Stalin informed a member of the Soviet-established Provisional Polish Government, Emil Somerstein, that Russia was interested in participating in the post-war settlement in the Middle East and that he was in favor of an international solution to the Jewish demands in Palestine. At the same time, Malenkov was even more emphatic by bluntly stating that the Jews should be given territory for a state in Palestine.[30]

The Yalta Conference made some interesting references to Palestine. Although information outside of the formal records is hard to substantiate, Yaacov Ro'i has insisted that the big three heads of state "agreed to the consolidation of the Jewish national home in Palestine and to the opening of that country's doors to Jewish immigration in the immediate future."[31]

The London Congress of Trade Unions

One of the first Soviet actions to implement a pro-Zionist stance was taken at the first London Congress of Trade Unions in February, 1945. The delegates claimed to speak for fifty million workers throughout the world. With the Soviet delegation's support, a special Zionist resolution was passed which stated:

> This convention is of the opinion that after the war a basic remedy must be found through international action to repair the evil done to the Jewish people. Protecting the Jews from oppression and discrimination, in any country, must be the obligation of the new international authority. The Jewish people must be given the opportunity to continue building up Palestine as their national home—an endeavour whose beginnings were crowned with success through immigration, agricultural settlement, and industrial development—while securing the just interests of all the population in it, and equal rights and opportunities for all.[32]

Support from the Trade Union International

Seven months later at the founding of the new Trade Union International by the 3,000 delegates representing some sixty million workers, the organization officially affirmed that "the Jewish people must be enabled to continue the upbuilding of Palestine as their national home through immigration, agricultural settlement, and industrial development;" although this policy was not to infringe upon "the interests of all the inhabitants of the country."[33] At a press conference, the Soviet representative reaffirmed his personal support for the resolution. Thus, while the Soviet position overtly affirmed support for the Jews in Palestine, that position had an element of naivete—in many ways similar to the British thinking in the interwar years—in that it assumed the support of Zionism could be achieved without antagonizing the major Arab groups or significantly curtailing what these groups felt were their legitimate interests.

Zionists of the Pro-Soviet Left

Individual pro-Soviet leaders of the Yishuv took the initiative in contacting Soviet officials to make their case. They developed rapport with members of the Soviet diplomatic missions in Europe, explaining to them the Soviet interest in helping to create the Jewish state in Palestine. They could make projections of a Soviet leaning, socialist state once independence was achieved. To the involved Jewish leaders such as Dr. Moshe Sneh (a founding member of the Mapam party and eventually secretary of the Israeli Communist party), Mordechai Oren (a leader of the left-wing Hashomer Hatzair party), Shmuel Mikunis (also a secretary of the Israeli Communist party), and Natan Peled (an official of Mapam), the future lay in looking toward the Soviet Union rather than the West. They effectively presented to the Soviets projections of a pro-Soviet state once independence was achieved. There is evidence to indicate that these dynamic Jewish leftists were a contributing factor in influencing Soviet policy toward the partition of Palestine[34]—an influence on policy which came through at the most crucial time of United Nations action on Palestine.

The Zionists' "Balance Sheet" after World War II

Viewed from the non-ideological, *real politique* perspective, the immediate post-World War II period found (1) the British solidly entrenched in the Middle East and (2) their economic situation gravely weakened. The Labor government under Attlee found it necessary to invite the United States to share the burden in some of Great Britain's worldwide commitments. British initiative got underway in 1946 and became urgent in early 1947 when the U.S. stepped in to accept responsibilities in Greece and Turkey in what became known as the Truman Doctrine. The Soviet Union was not happy to have a new American presence replacing that of a weakened Britain. To avoid drawing the Americans into the Arab Middle East as had happened in Greece, Turkey, and Iran, the Moscow government considered it preferable to promote its interests by supporting an independent Jewish state—especially in the situation of increasing Jewish antagonism to the British administration in Palestine.

In summary, at the end of World War II, Soviet Russia—as a major victorious power in the war—was in a much better position to influence the course of events in the Middle East than it had been after World War I. Nevertheless, American willingness to support Turkey and Iran with military force against a possible Soviet power thrust into the Middle East required the USSR to change tactics if its national interests were to be advanced. In the *immediate* post-war period, the Soviet Union—in spite of some pro-Arab, anti-Zionist proclamations—de-emphasized, for reasons stated above, its involvement in the Arab Middle East. At the same time, its policy gradually evolved into a low-keyed, low risk support for the Jewish leaders of Palestine—a policy which stemmed from both (1) common left-wing ideological considerations and the dynamic person-to-person contacts of personalities with roots in the same Russian culture and (2) objective political considerations on the part of the Soviets to support a low risk policy to get the British out—and perhaps to drive a wedge between the British and Americans.

Although Moscow frequently expressed condemnation of the Arab leaders at this time because of their cooperation with the imperialist governments of the West, there was the possibility that a bitter irreconcilable Arab-Jewish confrontation might develop into an opportunity. The United Nations might be required to send a peace-keeping force to Palestine. Peace-keeping was the primary responsibility of the Security

Council, which would increase Moscow's power to make its influence felt. With a veto over any action, the Soviet Union could effectively insist that its own military personnel be included in the Palestine force. (This kind of thinking turned out to be verified by later events—at least to the extent that the Arab-Israeli war did occur. In the Security Council debate of June 15, 1948, the Soviet Union pushed for the sending of its own military observers along with those of other states to restrain the Arab-Israeli hostilities. Sensing that Britain and the United States were obviously working to keep the Soviet troops out, Gromyko made a plea for only five Soviet military observers under the UN arrangement.[35])

To cover all eventualities and to avoid excessive Arab wrath beyond what the rational calculations of Soviet national interests required, Moscow also proclaimed its support of Arab independence movements. After World War II, it should be recalled, the Soviets supported the effective independence of Lebanon and Syria from French colonial ties. In 1947 the Soviet Union made it a point to give Egypt strong diplomatic support in the United Nations when that Middle East state appealed to the UN to get the British military forces out.

Egypt's July 8, 1947, request in the Security Council for the immediate and total British troop withdrawal from Suez, plus the later increased harassment by "hit and run" guerrilla tactics of the Egyptian nationalists, caused the British to search for other options in locating its major military base in the Middle East.

As already mentioned, in 1947 the British Foreign Office worked on plans to evacuate Egypt and retain Palestine; supplies and equipment were actually being moved from Egyptian military bases to El-Arish and Palestine.[36] This alternative the Russians were determined to stop, and the most feasible method involved terminating the British Mandatory relationship to Palestine by achieving some kind of viable independence for the area. Yet Palestine was a territory where the ability of the Arabs to provide for their own viability as a truly independent state was much more limited than in the surrounding states of Egypt, Lebanon, and Syria.

In this situation calling for new Soviet tactics, it is important to note that the politicization of the masses occurred not
among the Arabs but among the Jews. Ideologically, there was
still a strong communist or socialist sentiment among the intelligentsia of the east European immigrants to Palestine as expressed, for instance, in the kibbutz community organization.
"The kibbutz," noted Krammer, was "generally built on na-
tionally owned land and rented to the members on a communal basis." It was

> ... structured on the communal ownership of property, rotating
> leadership, self-sufficiency as a unit, disregard for money, and the
> equal distribution of the fruits of communal labor—"a society in
> which each gave according to his ability and in which each re-
> ceived according to his needs." By 1944, the editor-in-chief of the
> Palestine News Service, Eliahu Ben-Horin, could state that "in
> fact, Palestine can boast of better achievements in the field of
> economic communism than the Soviet Union."[37]

Thus, for the Soviets, the rising anti-British sentiment of this
Jewish "communist" social organization of the Yishuv could
and did become, at least momentarily, an attractive merger of
ideological and pragmatic national interest in the 1947–48
period when Arab political effectiveness was decidedly inferior and considered by the Soviet Union to be exploited in a
pro-British stance. The nationalist fervor of Zionism held
much higher prospects of success; the Soviets were not unaware of this fact. To summarize, the overall orientation of
Soviet policy toward the Middle East at this time was based on
the belief that it could work better with the more socialist,
progressive, (communist?), independent-minded Jews than
with the Arabs in getting the British out.

The Possibility of Britain's Veto

Yet in projecting a shift in policy toward the Jewish side
via support for partition, the Soviets were well aware of an

international political deadlock developing in the United Nations over the creation of Israel. Such a deadlock might well result in the stillbirth of the Jewish state and the continuation of the British presence in Palestine (or at least the kind of British sphere of influence that was to continue over Egypt for some time). Both Bartley Crum[38] and Jorge Garcia-Granados[39] relate personal experiences as members of the Palestine fact-finding commission which convinced them of the realistic possibility of a deadlock, through last minute maneuvering by the British Foreign Office, to block the Jewish efforts of statehood in Palestine.

NOTES

1. Walter Laqueur, *A History of Zionism* (New York: Holt, Rinehart and Winston, 1972), p. 263.

2. Walter Laqueur, *Communism and Nationalism in the Middle East* (New York: Praeger, 1956), notation 18, p. 97.

3. Ibid.

4. Ibid.

5. Laqueur, *Communism and Nationalism*, pp. 100, 108.

6. Ibid., p. 77.

7. Ibid., p. 75.

8. Ibid., p. 76.

9. Ibid.

10. Ibid., p. 78.

11. Richard Allen, *Imperialism and Nationalism in the Fertile Crescent* (London: Oxford University Press, 1974), p. 300. Note: Arnold Krammer (page 2 in *The Forgotten Friendship*. Urbana, Ill.: University of Illinois Press, 1974) reports 249 deaths. His figure apparently includes the Arabs killed by soldiers and police trying to restore order.

12. Laqueur, *Communism and Nationalism*, p. 85.

13. George Kirk, *A Short History of the Middle East*, 7th ed. (New York: Frederick Praeger, 1964), p. 154.

14. Laqueur, *Communism and Nationalism*, p. 104.

15. At the fifth party conference of the Palestine Communist party (July, 1924) a decisive anti-Zionist, anti-Jewish, and pro-Arab policy was adopted. Already in April it had been ousted from the Histadrut (the General Federation of Jewish Labour). Yet the Communist party membership was exclusively Jewish until the late 1920s and never achieved significant mass Arab support, although by 1934 the politburo had an Arab majority. See Laqueur, *Communism and Nationalism in the Middle East*, pp. 77–79, 87, 110. Later, two distinctive groupings of Palestine Communists came into existence. These were the so-called "Party Executive" and the "Jewish Section." The major point of antagonism was over the degree of support advocated for the Arab organized violence, 1936—39, as led by Hajj Amin el Husseini. See Laqueur, *op. cit.*, 300–301.

16. Laqueur, *Communism and Nationalism*, p. 112.

17. *Palestine Review*, September 1, 1941, p. 67. See also Cohen (as follows), p. 365.

18. Aharon Cohen, *Israel and the Arab World* (New York: Funk & Wagnalls, 1970), p. 360.

19. Ibid., p. 361.

20. Ibid.

21. Ibid., p. 360.

22. Ibid.

23. *Zionist Review*, August 28, 1942.

24. Ibid.

25. Cohen, p. 360.

26. Yaacov Ro'i, "Soviet-Israeli Relations, 1947–1954," *The U.S.S.R. in the Middle East*, eds. Michael Confino and Shimon Shamir (New York: John Wiley & Sons, 1973), pp. 123–124.

27. Cohen, pp. 361–362.

28. Bartley Crum, *Behind the Silken Curtain* (New York: Simon and Schuster, 1947), pp. 63–64. See also Cohen, pp. 362, 400.

29. Cohen, p. 363.

30. Yaacov Ro'i, "Soviet-Israeli Relations, 1947–1954," p. 123.

31. Ibid. Presumably this information was given to Dr. Stephen Wise by President Roosevelt a month before the latter's death. See Yaacov Ro'i, notation 5, p. 123.

32. "Proceedings of the first London Conference of Trade Unions," *Bahistadrut*, March, 1945, p. 13.

33. Cohen, pp. 363–364.

34. For an interesting discussion of the activities of these and other Jewish leaders, see: Arnold Krammer, *The Forgotten Friendship* (Urbana, Ill.: University of Illinois Press, 1974), pp. 34–39, 72–82.

35. United Nations Security Council, *Official Records, 320th Meeting,* 15 June 1948, pp. 6–7.

36. Elizabeth Monroe, *Britain's Moment in the Middle East 1914–1956* (London: Oxford, 1965), pp. 157, 158, and 165. See also Jaacov Ro'i, "Soviet-Israeli Relations, 1947–1954," p. 126.

37. Arnold Krammer, *The Forgotten Friendship* (Urbana, Ill.: University of Illinois Press, 1974), p. 49; as, in part quoting from: Alan D. Crown, "The Changing World of the Kibbutz," *The Middle East Journal*, autumn, 1965, p. 424. In the last sentence Krammer quotes: Eliahu Ben-Horin, "The Soviet Wooing of Palestine," *Harper's Magazine* 188 (April, 1944), 418.

38. Bartley Crum was appointed by President Roosevelt as one of the six American members who, along with six British nationals, constituted the 1946 Anglo-American Committee of Inquiry on Palestine. In his book, *Behind the Silken Curtain*, Crum is critical of the deceptive function the British intended for the Committee. Crum concludes that the British never were interested in an objective investigation of national self-determination possibilities; rather, the committee was intended as a subterfuge to rally U.S. support for the British objective of backing out of the Balfour Palestine commitment to the Jews. Crum concludes that Albert Einstein proved to be right when, contrary to the former's idealistic expectation, he characterized the committee's appointment as an intentional British device to delay action.

39. See Jorge Garcia-Granados' work, *The Birth of Israel* (New York: Alfred A. Knopf, 1949). As a member of UNSCOP (United Nations Special Committee On Palestine), Garcia-Granados was also very skeptical of the British intentions, charging them with ulterior motives to create a deadlock in the UN which would allow for continued British suzerainty in Palestine.

CHAPTER 4

Political Maneuvering in the United Nations

In January, 1947, Winston Churchill, now the leader of the opposition, made a speech in the House of Commons questioning the wisdom of Britain's continued role in Palestine. Great Britain had replaced Ottoman authority there as a result of the Allied victory in the First World War. Technically, it was the League of Nations which had given Britain the governing authority in the Palestine Mandate. British rule became increasingly turbulent in the inter-war years. From the very beginning there were charges that London had made mutually contradictory promises to the Jewish and Arab nationalists; each side insisted it had, with qualifications, been promised the land of Palestine—the Jews in the Balfour Declaration and the Arabs in the so-called Hussein-McMahan correspondence. The major difficulty for England arose, however, only after Hitler came to power in Germany and launched a program of anti-Semitism resulting in German Jews fleeing to Palestine—a situation helped along by the Western democracies having closed their doors to Jewish immigrants, except on a very selective basis.

Background Events Leading to UN Action

The Jewish Agency of Palestine found itself locking horns with the Palestine Arab leadership in three areas: (1) the right of Jews to immigrate to Palestine, (2) the right to buy land from Arabs, and (3) the objective of a separate Jewish state in Palestine in the areas of the Jewish settlements, but including some of the ancient Jewish religious sites—especially Jerusalem. The confrontation soon turned into a conflict with the British government, which increasingly sided with the Arabs against the Jews as Hitler and Mussolini initiated Axis expansion in the major dimensions of international politics.

In 1939 Great Britain declared its new Middle East policy in the so-called White Paper, which essentially sided with the Arabs in all three areas of Jewish-Arab conflict. Very shortly afterward, World War II exploded on the scene leaving the Zionists no alternative but to join their enemy, Britain, in supporting the war against Hitler's Germany, whose policy toward Jews was overwhelmingly worse than what the Jewish Agency experienced at the hands of Great Britain. From the latter's perspective, it could not afford to alienate the strategic Arab lands in this situation where the Axis partners were threatening Britain's very survival. After the war was over, the confrontation in Palestine resumed where it had left off.

The British Labor Party's victory in the July, 1945, elections had a rather unexpected impact on the Middle East. Labor had campaigned on a pro-Zionist platform, but immediately after Clement Attlee's government took over, the professional staff in the Foreign Office succeeded in convincing the new Labor leadership to oppose pro-Jewish measures which would alienate the Arabs. British imperial interests and the importance of oil made friendly relations with the Arabs imperative. Ernest Bevin, the new Foreign Secretary, decided on continuing, essentially, the strong anti-Zionist policy of the 1939 White Paper which was totally unacceptable to the Jews.

President Truman was much more sympathetic toward the Jews—although with reservations. In his *Memoirs* he insisted his policy was neither pro-Arab nor pro-Jew. Rather, American Middle East policy sought (1) to fulfill the Mandate promises to the Jews, (2) to relieve the suffering of Jews in war-torn Europe, and (3) to work out a solution through the United Nations.[1]

Nevertheless, shortly after the war in Europe was over,

Truman responded to Zionist concerns by urging Britain to immediately admit 100,000 Jews who were still languishing in the refugee camps of Europe. Bevin did not appreciate Truman's appeal. To take the heat off and perhaps change American policy, the British Foreign Secretary suggested a joint Anglo-American committee to investigate the problem. Truman accepted. Yet the committee's conclusion submitted to the British government several months later failed to align Washington's position with London; President Truman continued to press for the immediate admission of 100,000 Jews.

But to return to the developments in the UN in early 1947, we note that Jewish pressure for a "national homeland" was magnified due to the increased Arab opposition to the immigration of Jews to Palestine in the context of the irresistible determination of Jews to go there. Vivid memories of the death camps added to the Jewish sense of urgency.

Britian Turns Palestine over to the UN

Eventually the renewed Jewish determination, in conjunction with the large-scale erosion in Britain's economic position, created difficulties which the London government felt no longer warranted its continued role in Palestine. In February, 1947, British Foreign Secretary Bevin announced a governmental decision to turn the matter of the Palestine Mandate over to the United Nations.

The United Nations General Assembly met in its first special session in April to organize its own fact-finding procedures concerning Palestine so as to be in a position to dispose of the issue at its regular fall session. In the spring meeting, therefore, the General Assembly chose an eleven-member fact-finding committee (which excluded the big powers). This committee was called the United Nations Special Committee on Palestine (UNSCOP); its function was to conduct an extensive fact-finding mission and to make its recommendations to the United Nations General Assembly meeting in the fall.

Harry S. Truman

Harry S. Truman, the 33rd President of the United States. (Courtesy, Library of Congress)

Harry Truman, the 33rd President of the United States and a sharply partisan Democrat all his life, was born in 1884, the year Grover Cleveland won the Presidency and became the only Democratic President between the pre-Civil War Presidency of James Buchanan and the President of World War I, Woodrow Wilson.

Truman was born at Lamar, a small country town twenty miles from the Kansas border in southwestern Missouri. His father failed as a mule trader, which sent the Truman family on the move. At age three, Truman and his family took up residence with Harry's maternal grandparents, and the father, John, took over the farming operations.

In 1890 the Trumans inherited a modest share of the Anderson Truman estate, which made it possible to move to Independence (on the eastern edge of Kansas City) where the six-year-old Harry could have the benefit of better schools. Although basically a healthy child, the parents soon learned that their son would need thick eyeglasses to cope with severe hyperopia and "flat eyeballs." Thus, on the playlot he was relegated to be "the umpire" instead of participating in the game. Later it also kept him out of West Point and Annapolis. The disappointment was re-channelled into vicariously living the great moments of history by his voracious reading—particularly biographies of great men. He had a special admiration for Presidents Andrew Jackson and Woodrow Wilson. It has been suggested that his physical handicap made the Presidency possible—the glasses kept him out of sports and farm boy activities long enough to get an education through reading.

During World War I he enlisted and fought with the American forces in France as an artillery officer. By the end of 1919 two important events had occurred. He married Bess Wallace, his acquaintance since they first attended the Presbyterian Sunday school together at Independence in 1890; and he and Eddie Jacobson (his old buddy from Battery F) decided to open a men's clothing shop in downtown Kansas City—a business which lasted only a few years until it went bankrupt.

Truman then turned to politics. Backed by the

Pendergast "political machine," he was elected county judge in 1922. In the 1930s his strong support for Franklin D. Roosevelt paid off when he won the 1934 election as U. S. Senator from Missouri. Senator Truman soon developed a reputation for honesty and effectiveness as chairman of the Senate War Investigating Committee checking corruption and inefficiencies in the huge American defense program of World War II. It is also true that he had to live down the stigma of previous association with the infamous Pendergast machine of Kansas City.

In the 1944 elections he stumbled into the Vice-Presidency when the Democratic bosses became alarmed at Roosevelt's deteriorating health and abhorred the thought of Henry Wallace becoming President.

Harry Truman's greatest moments in history include his sudden swearing in as President of the United States upon the death of Roosevelt on April 12, 1945; the decision to drop the atomic bombs on Japan; prosecuting the war to its successful conclusion over Germany and Japan; standing up to Soviet expansion after World War II; sending American forces to stop North Korean aggression in 1950; and fighting inflation in the turbulent American economy after World War II.

In reference to the Middle East, not only did he succeed in halting Soviet pressures by aid to Greece and Turkey, President Truman was crucially involved in the creation of Israel. It was Truman's former clothing store partner, Eddie Jacobson, who changed the President's mind and arranged to have him meet Chaim Weizmann, the most effective spokesman for the creation of Israel. It is said with considerable credibility that had it not been for Truman's support, the state of Israel would not have been created.

Harry Truman decided not to seek re-election in 1952. He died on December 26, 1972.

UNSCOP presented its recommendations to the Second Regular Session of the General Assembly in two major resolutions. By unanimous vote, the eleven-member committee recommended the termination of Britain's administration of Palestine. By majority vote, UNSCOP proposed a partition of Palestine with separate Jewish and Arab states, although the recommendation advocated a common market (economic union) between the two states. Jerusalem, furthermore, was to be a permanent Trust Territory under the United Nations.

The Soviet Surprise

It was this agenda item which provided the context for Andrei Gromyko's startling pro-Jewish speech of November 26 (quoted previously) and the Soviet support for the creation of Israel in the General Assembly vote of November 29—a resolution passed by a vote of 33 to 13 with 10 abstentions.

How did the Soviets engineer this striking switch in policy? As late as February 8, 1947, *Izvestia* still emphasized the pro-Arab, anti-partition theme. In an article under the by-line of "Observer," entitled "On International Themes,"[2] the proposed British plan for the partition of Palestine into an autonomous Jewish state as well as an autonomous Arab state (plus two directly ruled British areas) was sharply criticized. "It is no accident," said the Soviet voice, "that many observers connect the plan for partition of Palestine with British schemes for the creation of a so-called Eastern bloc . . . " The British partition plan, said *Izvestia*, does not take into account "the aspirations and wishes of the Arab peoples, and by not taking these into account, it leads to threats of violence."

Three months later a noticeable change in Soviet policy toward the Jewish objective of partition (an objective which was totally condemned by the Arabs) had occurred. Andrei Gromyko, speaking in the plenary session of the First Special Session of the United Nations General Assembly, for the first time gave conditional Soviet support for partition!

Gromyko presented a sympathetic account of Jewish suffering at the hands of the Nazi regime during World War II:

> During the last war, the Jewish people underwent exceptional sorrow and suffering. Without any exaggeration, this sorrow and suffering are indescribable. It is difficult to express them in dry statistics on the Jewish victims of the fascist aggressors. The Jews in territories where the Hitlerites held sway were subjected to almost complete physical annihilation. The total number of members of the Jewish population who perished at the hands of the nazi [sic] executioners is estimated at approximately six million. Only about a million and a half Jews in Western Europe survived the war. . . .

> The fact that no western European State has been able to ensure the defence of the elementary rights of the Jewish people, and to safeguard it against the violence of the fascist executioners, explains the aspirations of the Jews to establish their own State. It would be unjust not to take this into consideration and to deny the right of the Jewish people to realize this aspiration. It would be unjustifiable to deny this right to the Jewish people, particularly in view of all it has undergone during the Second World War.

Gromyko continued by emphasizing the moral responsibility of the United Nations to help the Jews:

> The time has come to help these people, not by word, but by deeds. It is essential to show concern for the urgent needs of a people which has undergone such great suffering as a result of the war brought about by Hitlerite Germany. This is a duty of the United Nations.

Then he expressed the Soviet Union's proposed solution:

> . . . The solution of the Palestine problem by the establishment of a single Arab-Jewish State with equal rights for the Jews and Arabs may be considered as one of the possibilities. . . .

> If this plan proved impossible to implement, in view of the deterioration in the relations between the Jews and the Arabs . . .

then it would be necessary to consider the second plan which . . . provides for the partition of Palestine into two independent autonomous States, one Jewish and one Arab.[3]

Zionists Grateful to the UN

The November 29 (1947) UN action of partition was an emotional event for the Zionists. What had earlier seemed impossible was now a real opportunity. Yet it was only an opportunity; the big powers might change their minds; an even greater challenge existed in the fact that a Jewish state would come into being only if the Yishuv could militarily defend itself from the wrath of the Arabs.

The Yishuv's Frantic Efforts to Acquire Weapons

Immediately after the UN action of November 29, the Haganah (Jewish defense force) expanded its efforts to find arms. Weapons would be crucial in the expected confrontation with Arab armies which, with the exception of Lebanon and Syria, were trained and supplied with weapons by the British. Considerable amounts of World War II military equipment remained scattered all over the world; with hard currency it was relatively easy to acquire, although it usually required ingenuity to smuggle the material across national boundaries. The Haganah was able to secretly get weapons from many sources, yet its major purchases were clandestinely arranged with the approval of the Soviet Union. The operation was fraught with difficulties. The state of Israel had not yet come into existence. British and American governments put pressure on other states to keep them from selling to the Jews or allowing the transportation of these arms across their territories. The British administration in Palestine renewed its efforts to intercept arms smuggled into the area. Money (hard currency) was always in short supply as far as the Haganah was concerned. Golda Meir was sent on a special fund-raising trip to the United States to acquire money for arms.

Of interest to us here is the fact that the major source of arms for Israel was the Soviet-approved weapons purchases in Czechoslovakia. Beginning on December 1, 1947, and using the cover of official Ethiopian government stationery (purchased at the average cost of ten dollars a sheet), Ehud Avriel of the Haganah made the first purchase of surplus German arms (originally manufactured in Czechoslovakia for the Wehrmacht) from a Skoda official in Prague.[4]

Arnold Krammer lists the following amounts of weapons purchased through February, 1949, at Prague with unofficial Soviet approval:[5]

57,000,000	rounds of 7.92 mm. ammunition
1,500,000	rounds of 9 mm. Parabellum ammunition
1,000,000	rounds of anti-tank ammunition
24,500	P-18 Mauser rifles
10,000	bayonets for the P-18 Mauser rifle
5,015	(Light) ZB-34 Machine-guns
880	(Heavy) ZB-37 Machine-guns
250	9 mm. Zbrojovka pistols
12	16-ton tanks with ammunition
10	9.5-ton tanks with ammunition
25	Avia-Messerschmitt 109 (S-199) fighter planes
59	Spitfire IX fighter planes
4,184	2-kg. bombs
2,988	10-kg. bombs
146	20-kg. bombs
2,614	70-kg. bombs

The Jewish "International Brigade"

While the Soviet-approved project of secretly supplying arms to Israel was taking place, a startling new development in Czech aid to Israel occurred. The Jewish leftist, Shmuel

Mikunis, approached the Prague government after the February, 1948, Communist coup and sought permission to recruit and train a "Czech brigade" to help the Jews fight the Arabs.[6] Historical precedents were not hard to find. The most recent examples were the international brigades sent to fight in the Spanish civil war. Israel (1) was desperately in need of trained soldiers and (2) saw this as a means by which Czech Jews would be able to immigrate to Palestine.

Mikunis' request was approved by no less a Soviet official than Malenkov, who contacted Mikunis in a midnight telephone call on June 20, 1948.[7] In spite of the fact that the project came to an abrupt end in November, 1948, as a result of United States pressure on the Czech government,[8] approximately a thousand Czech volunteers (mostly Jews) were trained at the old Czech army base at Velke-Schelba, Bohemia.[9] The brigade was organized by the non-Jew, Major General Antonin Sochor,[10] who had received the Hero of the Soviet Union award for distinguished military service in World War II.

Unfortunately for Israel, the last contingent of the brigade didn't arrive in Israel until February, 1949—when the war was almost over.

The Prague officials had pressed for the right to have the Czech brigade participate in the war as a unit—even bringing in additional members of the Haganah in Israel who were of Czech background. This proposal was unacceptable to Israel. As Haganah Commander Itzhak Shany remarked, there was a grave potential danger for Israel in the situation of a self-contained fighting unit in the Israel army being commanded by a Communist officer "whose first loyalty was to Prague"[11] and, one might add, ultimately controlled by Moscow.

Why was the Communist Prague government willing to secretly promote the fortunes of Israel to this extent? The answer is fourfold:[12] (1) The Czech government wanted to get rid of its Jews, who were potential trouble-makers for the regime. (2) It was good public relations to get rid of the Jews under the noble banner of cooperation with the requests of Israel. (3)

The domestic political composition of Israel would be more favorably disposed toward Czechoslovakia. (4) It would enrich the state because all possessions of the Czech emigrants were taken over by the government without compensation.

U.S. Policy in the UN

In early 1948 President Truman was backing off from too close support of the Jewish objectives in Palestine. He became annoyed at the Jewish requests which flooded the White House; Truman instructed his staff not to grant appointments for Jewish lobbyists to see him. He even rejected an appointment request from Dr. Chaim Weizmann, the most sophisticated and prestigious spokesman for the Zionist cause. It was in this situation that Eddie Jacobson, Truman's old buddy in World War I and his former business partner in the ill-fated men's clothing store in Kansas City, appeared at the White House for a visit on March 13, 1948. Mr. Jacobson was a practicing Jew, but not a Zionist.

As Truman relates the incident:

> I was always glad to see him. Not only had we shared so much in the past, but I have always had the warmest feelings toward him. It would be hard to find a truer friend. Eddie said that he wanted to talk about Palestine. I told him that I would rather he did not and that I wanted to let the matter run its course in the United Nations.[13]

But Mr. Jacobson was determined not to drop the matter.

> Eddie waved toward a small replica of an Andrew Jackson statue that was in my office.
> "He's been your hero all your life, hasn't he?" he said. "You have probably read every book there is on Andrew Jackson. I remember when we had the store that you were always reading books and pamphlets, and a lot of them were about Jackson. You put this statue in front of the Jackson County Courthouse in Kansas City when you built it."

I did not know what he was leading up to, but he went on.

"I have never met the man who has been my hero all my life," he continued. "But I have studied his past as you have studied Jackson's. He is the greatest Jew alive, perhaps the greatest Jew who ever lived."[14]

Mr. Jacobson then pushed his point home by telling Harry that it just "isn't like you" to turn away a "very sick man" of Weizmann's stature who had traveled thousands of miles to see him. Truman then agreed to see Chaim Weizmann.

The secret White House meeting did take place five days later (March 18). Weizmann emphasized the great potential of Jews in developing and industrializing Palestine and the importance of including the Negev in the future Jewish state as living space for the masses of worldwide Jewry who would be immigrating to their newly established homeland. President Truman felt the visit had gone well and that there had been a meeting of minds on the substantive issues discussed.[15]

However, a basic political dilemma remained. Truman had to deal with the Jewish demands for an independent state in the face of increasing State Department pressures to abandon partition and support the British appeal for continued UN Trusteeship for Palestine. Truman was still undecided on the issue when, the day after the Weizmann visit, American representative to the UN, Ambassador Warren Austin, announced in the Security Council (March 19) a reversal of American policy on Palestine. The United States, said Austin, no longer supported the partition of Palestine; instead, he suggested a UN trusteeship to replace the British Mandate which had originally been created by the League of Nations after World War I. Thus he proposed the calling of a special session of the General Assembly to rescind its partition policy and to replace it with a continued UN responsibility under a "temporary" trust arrangement—a position much more acceptable to the Arabs. In reaction to this reversal of American policy the Soviet delegate, Andrei Gromyko, responded by charging the United States with resorting to the subtle self-interest of oil and continued domination of a colonial Middle East.

The Security Council then took action by voting unanimously for a ceasefire resolution and voting 9-0-2 (the Soviet Union and the Ukraine abstaining) on a second resolution calling for the above-mentioned special session of the General Assembly.[16]

President Truman was furious at Austin. In his diary entry for March 19 he recorded the disaster as follows:

> "The State Dept. pulled the rug from under me today. I didn't expect that would happen. In Key West . . . I approved the speech and statement of policy by Senator Austin to U.N. meeting. This morning I find that the State Dept. has reversed my Palestine policy. The first I know about it is what I see in the paper! Isn't that hell? I am now in the postion of a liar and a double-crosser. I've never felt so in my life.
>
> "There are people on the third and fourth levels of the State Dept. who have always wanted to cut my throat. They've succeeded in doing it."[17]

Mrs. Eleanor Roosevelt submitted her resignation as a member of the American UN delegation in protest. Only the President's personal plea to stay on changed her mind. Margaret Truman (the President's daughter) referred to the incident as "one of the worst messes of my father's career, and he could do nothing about it but suffer."[18]

President Truman finally rationalized the fiasco to the press by emphasizing that partition was still America's policy; the trusteeship arrangement was intended only for a short interim.

Any account of the sudden change in American policy toward Palestine must include an examination of the factors that were instrumental in effecting this change.

On February 16 (1948) the United Nations Palestine Commission had warned the Security Council that it would be unable to carry out its UN responsibility of insuring respect for the UN partition boundaries unless the United Nations made "military forces in adequate strength" available to it. In fairness to the position held by the State Department group, the

Arabs and Jews were on collision course in Palestine; the threat of a very bloody confrontation was probable. If this were allowed to happen, irresistible pressure might well be put on the UN to send in a military force to stop the blood letting—a situation in which the United States would find it difficult to keep Soviet troops out of a United Nations Palestine force militarily strong enough to keep order. The State Department had to deal with the situation within the constraints of (1) President Truman's determination that no American troops should be sent to the area unless the Arabs and the Jews first agreed to a truce (a very unlikely case) and (2) the failure of U.S. efforts to get smaller countries such as Belgium, Brazil, Netherlands, Norway, and Denmark to provide an effective military force.[19]

Furthermore, it became very difficult to work out a consistent, rational, and effective American policy toward the Middle East when more urgent national issues distracted State Department efforts in this area of the world. At this time, priority demands included (1) the rising cold war embodying (a) the Marshall Plan, (b) the Czech takeover, (c) the Berlin crisis; (2) the Italian peace treaty and the crucial Italian elections of April, 1948; (3) the major domestic political issue—the post-World War II *inflation*; and (4) the Presidential election of 1948. In the UN, therefore, the United States now pushed for the creation of a provisional international trusteeship for Palestine under the United Nations.

Plans called for it to be administered by the British for the United Nations, since the United States consistently followed a policy of preventing Soviet personnel from participating in any United Nations-involved political activity in Palestine. On April 20, 1948, the United States carried its new policy position to the General Assembly. It reflected a growing American concern, on behalf of the military, about the rapidly deteriorating East-West relations resulting from politically destabilizing events in both Europe and the Far East. As the State Department and the military leaders in Washington saw the issues, increasingly clear U.S. interests dictated the advisability of the new policy against the partition of Palestine—a partition which was totally unacceptable to the Arab world. The changed policy was defended by the State Department professionals along the following lines: (1) partition could not be achieved peacefully, (2) the Security Council had no military or police force at its disposal, (3) only the major powers could provide the military forces needed to avoid bloodshed, (4) the Russians would demand equal participation in any United Nations military force used in Palestine, and (5) the physical presence of Soviet troops in Palestine might never be withdrawn or might not be limited to UN determined purposes. The U.S. military insisted that Palestine must be available as a base for Western ground and air forces in view of the developing East-West conflict.[20]

Since it would probably be impossible to put U.S. troops into Palestine without Soviet troops, Austin proposed that British troops should remain in Palestine to deal with the rising threat of all-out war. Furthermore, Austin's backing away from partition in favor of a UN Trust of indefinite duration served to reduce Arab antagonism toward the Western Middle East policy since World War II. This was especially important to the Western democracies in the situation of the rising cold war.

It was this U.S. demand for continued British troops to control the politics of Palestine and enforce law and order under a United Nations Trusteeship that antagonized the Russians and verified their previously stated contention that, in reality, Britain's imperialistic ties to the Levant would not easily be given up.[21] Moscow viewed this development as another typical British maneuver in a whole series of acts, beginning with Great Britain's active encouragement of the creation of the Arab League (March, 1945)—to retain, as seen by the Soviets, control and influence in the post-war Middle East. Furthermore, as discussed above, the British strategy of attempting to move its big Suez base from Egypt to Palestine was considered by Moscow as another example of this kind of English tenacity in holding on to the Middle East.

The Soviets were increasingly apprehensive upon receiving news of yet another British plan to maximize London's influence in the Middle East at the Yishuv's expense. This was the British "Clayton Plan" which was devised by Brig. Charles Clayton, one of Britain's top Middle East strategists. The plan called for Syria (and perhaps Lebanon) to take over Galilee and most of northern Palestine; Egypt would be given the Negev desert, and King Abdullah (Jordan) would be given permission to send in his "Arab Legion" to take over most of the region in between (including Hebron, Jericho, Jerusalem, and Gaza). The Jewish state would be limited to a coastal strip from Tel Aviv to Haifa. This would make it possible for the British military forces to develop an effective line of communication from Jordan through Jericho, Jerusalem to Gaza on the coast.[22] The Jews, however, found this scheme no more acceptable than the Bernadotte Plan developed later in September (1948). The Bernadotte proposal strongly favored the Arabs and was "vetoed" by the Jews in the assassination of the United Nations' Mediator, Count Folke Bernadotte.

Soviet projections of American policy must have received another jolt when President Truman took revenge on the pro-Arab State Department professionals (whose position was represented by Warren Austin in his March 19 statement) and announced U.S. recognition of Israel eleven minutes after David Ben-Gurion proclaimed the existence of the new state in Palestine (May 14, 1948).[23]

Now, the Zionist Jews were in ecstasy and the Arab leaders were furious. Moscow was relieved, although perhaps a little ambivalent because Washington had beaten the Soviets to the recognition of Israel. Expressions of appreciation for the speedy recognition flooded the White House. David Niles of the Truman administration relates a moving incident of thanksgiving when Israel's Chief Rabbi (Herzog) paid a visit to Truman a year after Israel's creation:

"Rabbi Herzog told Truman, 'God put you in your mother's womb so you would be the instrument to bring about the rebirth of Israel

David Ben-Gurion

Prime Minister David Ben-Gurion (center) in his office in Jerusalem, December 1, 1953, presenting to Moshe Dayan (second from right) the flag of the Chief of Staff symbolizing Mr. Dayan's appointment to that office effective December 6. Foreign Minister Moshe Sharett is on the extreme right. (Courtesy, The Embassy of Israel)

David Ben-Gurion was born December 16, 1886, into a family already committed to Zionism. His birthplace at Plonsk was at the time a part of Russia. Poland was resurrected again after World War I, and Plonsk, located some 35 miles northwest of Warsaw, became a part of the new Poland. David was the sixth of eleven children born to Avigdor and Sheindel Green. The future prime minister of Israel changed his surname from Green to Ben-Gurion in 1910. As a teenager, the "father of modern Israel," the great Jewish leader who eventually learned to speak nine languages, immigrated to Palestine in 1906 and went to work as a manual laborer to build Zion.

To Ben-Gurion, Zionism included the call to immigrate to Palestine, the ancient land of the Hebrews, as well as to use the Hebrew language in the daily life of the Jewish community. He also emphasized the importance of Jewish physical labor in building the agricultural base of a future Jewish state.

At this time Palestine was a part of the Ottoman Empire, and the young emigrant from Plonsk was optimistic about establishing rapport with the autocratic government at Istanbul. This seemed especially appealing after the Young Turk revolution in 1908. Ben-Gurion had aspirations of winning a seat in the new parliament, which could be of great benefit to the Yishuv (Jewish community) in Palestine. That hope was never realized, but together with his close friend, Isaac Ben-Zvi, Ben-Gurion enrolled at the Ottoman University in Istanbul to study Turkish law—to be successful in confrontation with the Ottoman officials, the police, and the effendis. In buying land and gaining rights for the Jewish community, he would have to be able to win at their own game.

When World War I broke out and Turkey became the enemy of the Western powers, Ben-Gurion was expelled as a potential enemy. Eventually he made his way to the United States where he contacted Louis D. Brandeis (whom President Wilson, later in 1916, appointed to the U. S. Supreme Court) to help get permission for the recruitment of Americans to join the Jewish legion which was organized by the British. This Jewish volunteer force was attached to the British military force under General Allenby's command. Ben-Gurion became an officer in the Fortieth Battalion of the Royal Fusiliers.

In November, 1917, Great Britain issued the Balfour Declaration. David Ben-Gurion immediately realized that a Jewish national home in Palestine would become a reality only if Jews immigrated there and made it their land by draining the swamps, planting the orchards, and building the community. After the war, he set out to create a Jewish organization to serve this role—to be the forerunner of a Jewish state. This was done in 1921 in the creation of the *Histadrut* (General Federation of Labour in Palestine). From 1921 to 1933 he was general secretary of the organization. He assumed leadership of the Mapai political party, which later headed the first government of Israel. In 1933 he became a member of the executive board of the Jewish Agency, and two years later became chairman of this governing body of the Jewish community in Palestine.

The increased Arab antagonism to Jewish immigration after Hitler's rise to power in Germany, plus the threat of general war in Europe, caused Britain to issue its White Paper of 1939—a severe blow to Jewish aspirations for their own state in Palestine. As a spokesman for the Zionists, Ben-Gurion responded to the new British policy and the outbreak of World War II by stating that the Jews would "fight the war as if there were no White Paper and the White Paper as if there were no war."

No individual has been more instrumental in the creation and the continued existence of the state of Israel than David Ben-Gurion. It was he who formally proclaimed the new state on May 14, 1948, serving as its first Prime Minister and Minister of Defense. In December, 1953, he resigned from government and, as a private citizen, joined the kibbutz at Sde Boker in the Negev. In February, 1955, he returned to government as Minister of Defense following the infamous "Lavon Affair." He again became Prime Minister in July, 1955, and ended his distinguished service as head of Israel's government by resigning again in June, 1963.

Ben-Gurion made many secret contacts with Arab leaders to settle the prolonged Palestine conflict. He was, however, a hard liner in advocating sharp retaliation for violent Arab incidents against Israel. Israel fought its first two wars under his government's direction.

He died December 1, 1973—two weeks before his

eighty-seventh birthday. The trauma of the early defeats in the Yom Kippur War had had its impact on the old warrior. He died relieved that the Israeli military forces, which he had helped create, had once more prevailed.

---

after two thousand years.' I thought he was overdoing things, but when I looked over at the President, tears were running down his cheeks."[24]

When President Truman personally selected James G. McDonald, noted for his pro-Jewish position, to head the first U.S. diplomatic mission to Israel in June, 1948—which Truman planned as a Class I Mission—Robert Lovett, then Undersecretary of State and representing very much the pro-Arab bureaucracy of the Department, shared his feelings with Mr. McDonald in projecting it as a Class IV Mission.[25] Without the frequent direct intervention of President Truman, due to his personal interest in the matter, the more pro-Arab oriented career officers of the State Department would very probably have swung American policy into a position considerably different from that established under the President's direction.

Proposal to Reduce Israel's Territory

Getting the British out of Palestine came to be a major objective for Soviet Middle East policy. Even in the Western democracies, certain anti-colonial voices were very skeptical about the likelihood of Great Britain giving up its position in the crucially-located area of Palestine. For instance, the pro-Israeli U.S. Ambassador to Israel, James McDonald, saw the events of Count Bernadotte's assassination in the context of British reluctance to accept the erosion of its position in the Levant through the creation of Israel. As already mentioned,

Count Bernadotte, the UN's Mediator in Palestine, tried to deal with the military stalemate during the first Arab–Israeli war by reducing Israel's territory from that set forth in the United Nations' earlier plans. His proposal required Israel to give up the southern desert of Palestine—called the Negev—in exchange for a smaller area of Western Galilee which had already been taken by Jewish arms. Bernadotte was assassinated on September 17 by a Jewish terrorist organization. His pro-Arab plan was then strongly pushed by the British, and the U.S. Secretary of State Marshall formally accepted the plan as a fair basis for dealing with the turn of events. Ambassador McDonald commented on the situation by saying that the British Foreign Office Officials

> had been highly pleased with the Mediator's ideas, for his plan assured Jordan control—that is, British control—of the Negev, the much-wanted "land bridge" from Egypt to Jordan. It also reduced Israel both territorially and psychologically to more manageable proportions. Bevin with great satisfaction therefore hurled his indictment against Israel and sought to rally support for the hurried adoption by the United Nations of all Bernadotte proposals.[26]

To elaborate, U.S. Secretary of State Marshall gave American support for the retention of British influence in the area by approving the late Mediator's proposals and urging "the UN General Assembly and the countries directly concerned to 'accept them in their entirety as the best possible means of bringing peace' " to Palestine.[27] In fairness to Marshall's position, one notes the obviously broader perspective to which the Secretary had to relate. At this time (1948) a major escalation of the cold war was taking place, including extremely dangerous tensions in Berlin (the Berlin Airlift). Europe was, after all, the priority in American foreign policy concerns. If necessary, objectives in the Middle East were expendable. Containment considerations became very important, and the Arabs, not Israel, held the trump card here. This created a sense of urgency for the United States and Britain to reconcile differences with the Arab Middle East if possible.

By 1947–48 the British Foreign Office and the U.S. Department of State were aware of Soviet strategy to exploit differences between the Western Allies which would facilitate Moscow's expansion into the Middle East. Nevertheless, a pro-Jewish policy carried very significant weight in the United States domestic politics, and 1948 was a presidential election year—an election which Truman was determined to win.

NOTES

1. Harry S. Truman, *Memoirs*, vol. 2 (Garden City, N. Y.: Doubleday and Co., 1956), p. 160.

2. Observer, "On International Themes," *Izvestia*, February 8, 1947, p. 4.

3. United Nations General Assembly, 77th Plenary Meeting, May 14, 1947, *Discussion of the Report of the First Committee on the Establishment of a Special Committee on Palestine* (A/307/Corr. 1), pp. 131, 132, and 134.

4. Arnold Krammer, *The Forgotten Friendship* (Urbana, Ill.: University of Illinois Press, 1974), p. 60.

5. Ibid., pp. 105–106.

6. Ibid., p. 107.

7. Ibid.

8. Ibid., p. 111.

9. Ibid., p. 110.

10. Ibid., p. 109

11. Ibid., p. 110.

12. Ibid., p. 108.

13. Truman, p. 160.

14. Ibid., p. 161.

15. Ibid.

16. *New York Times*, April 4, 1948, IV, p. 2.

17. Margaret Truman, *Harry S. Truman* (New York: William Morrow and Co., 1973), p. 388.

18. Ibid., p. 389.

19. *New York Times*, April 18, 1948, IV. p. 1.

20. Welles, pp. 81–82.

21. See the Ukraninian delegate's speech of May 14, 1948, in the United Nations: *Official Records of the 2nd Special Session of the General Assembly*, pp. 257–258.

22. *New York Times*, April 18, 1948, IV, p. 5.

23. Truman, p. 164.

24. Alfred Steinberg, *The Man from Missouri: The Life and Times of Harry Truman* (New York: G. P. Putnam's Sons, 1962), p. 308.

25. James C. McDonald, *My Mission in Israel*, 1948–1951 (New York: Simon and Schuster, 1951), p. 12.

26. Ibid., p. 85.

27. Ibid., p. 84.

CHAPTER 5

The Political Environment of Soviet Middle East Policy: The East-West Confrontation and Soviet Domestic Politics

On May 7, 1945, Germany's aggression had been turned into defeat. The threat to Soviet survival was over. Moscow was understandably exuberant in victory. The Soviet Union's major role in victory would have to be acknowledged in re-creating the international political order. It would not be a World War I settlement when, in 1919, the new government was on the defensive simply to survive after being defeated in war and threatened by White Russian armies abetted by the Western democracies. At the time, the Western allies of World War I were very unhappy with the new revolutionary Soviet regime which had seized power and taken Russia out of the war.

The East-West Confrontation

In March, 1945, the Soviet government unilaterally denounced its treaty of friendship with Turkey, and in June it demanded a naval base on the Dardanelles plus the two eastern Turkish provinces of Kars and Ardahan. Six months earlier an indirect demand had already been made for a 200 mile slice of eastern Turkey.[1]

In Iran the Soviets used their wartime occupation status in the north to support separatist movements in the Azerbaijan and Kurdistan areas of northern Iran. The Soviet Union was instrumental in December, 1945, in establishing the Autonomous Republic of Azerbaijan and the Kurdish Peoples' Republic. Soviet troops protected their puppets from the Iranian forces sent by the Teheran government to re-assert Iranian sovereignty over the area. Through United States determination to support Iran, and by pressure in the United Nations, the Russians finally decided to abandon Iranian territories—but on the condition of receiving oil exploration concessions. (The oil concession treaty was signed, but after the withdrawal of Soviet troops, the Iranian Majlis (legislature) voted not to ratify it.)

The Soviet Union also demanded "spoils" in the Arab Muslim world. At the mid-July, 1945, summit conference at Potsdam, Stalin expressed interest in acquiring the "trust territories" of the former Italian territories of Libya and Eritrea. Later in September a formal request was made for the trust territory of Tripolitania (the most important section of Libya). Eritrea was formally requested by Molotov in April at the 1946 Conference of Foreign Ministers in Paris. This would facilitate Soviet national interests with regard to the Suez Canal, the Indian Ocean, and the hinterland of Ethiopia. The Soviet Union also demanded the Dodecanese Islands for a naval base to protect the approaches to the Straits.

Nevertheless, the highest priority for Soviet national interests was a favorable settlement in central Europe. Areas occupied by Soviet troops would not easily be relinquished to a truly independent state. The "victors falling out among the spoils" would form the most intense pressure in Germany.

Conflict Over Germany

In Germany, any hope of terminating the separate occupation zones by the creation of a united Germany tended to fade when the Western democracies decided, in May, 1946, to halt the removal from their zones of German equipment being shipped to Russia as reparations. As the West saw it, unless they were willing to let the German population of their zones undergo severe deprivation—a revolutionary situation which the Soviets could readily exploit—they would have to replace the German equipment with equipment from the United States. With the increasing antagonism developing in relations with the Soviets, this kind of subsidy was no longer tolerable. The Soviet Union, however, insisted that it was entitled to receive the large-scale German reparations to rebuild its war-shattered economy.

Failure, again, to reach an East-West accommodation at the next foreign ministers' conference (London, November 15 to December 15, 1947) resulted in a British–United States move toward unifying their respective zones of occupation. Later, the French authorities joined in creating trizonal cooperation in opposition to the Soviet occupation zone in Germany.

With reparations out of the Western zones halted, the Soviets were still left with one other means of squeezing economic assets out of the Western occupation zone, namely, the inflation, in their zone, of the common currency for all Germany. However, the Allied monetary reform which created new currency for exclusive use only in the Western zone eliminated the last avenue for the Soviets to economically exploit the West in Germany. The Soviets responded politically with the extremely dangerous blockade of the Western surface access routes to Berlin. In turn, the West responded with the famous Berlin airlift in June, 1948.

Not only did the Soviets want resources to rebuild what the war had destroyed in Russia; economic resources were necessary for the urgently felt need to eliminate the Western monopoly on atomic weapons.

The Creation of the Soviet Satellite System

In central Europe, in the wake of their military conquests of World War II, the Soviets set up subservient Communist governments, attaching them politically, ideologically, and economically to the "Socialist fatherland." These included Poland, Czechoslovakia, Hungary, Rumania, Bulgaria, and the Soviet occupation zone of Germany—East Germany. (In certain other territories, attempts were made to set up a potential for later expansion by building an enclave or organizing strong support for a local Communist party which could be directed from Moscow. Examples of the latter included Greece, Iran, and Manchuria.)

In retrospect, it now seems Stalin felt the great victory of Soviet arms (although by the narrowest of margins in 1941–42 and by the sacrifice of millions of nationals) was a moment of destiny. Now was the hour for historical fulfillment.

The Soviets' destiny for Poland was already being promoted in mid-1944 when they created the Lublin Committee and granted to it political authority over territory recaptured by the Soviet army from the German forces. A year earlier Moscow had broken diplomatic relations with the Polish Government in Exile based in London. At the Yalta Conference, Stalin agreed to the Western demands to include members of both the London government and the Polish resistance leaders in broadening the base of the newly established Polish government. However, a Polish government subservient to Moscow was not to be denied. Polish leaders from the underground and from the pro-Allied government of London— leaders who were named to join the new Soviet-created government according to the Yalta agreement—were jailed and many executed.

By V-E Day (May 7, 1945) the Soviets had similarly taken over Rumania, in spite of the Yalta agreement pledging the creation of democratic institutions by the Rumanians' own choice. On that day they signed an agreement with "the government of Rumania" establishing joint control over many of the country's natural resources. Earlier (February 27, 1945) the king had been given a four hour ultimatum to create a government for Rumania composed of men picked by Moscow. Although a brief hassle with the West ensued, the result followed the pattern established in Poland. All party organizations except the Communists were destroyed and opposition jailed or executed. The Rumanian king finally capitulated in December, 1947. Rumania officially became a People's Democracy on the pattern demanded by the Soviet Union in April, 1948.

The Soviet Army took over Bulgaria in September, 1944. Until 1945 the Soviets allowed a coalition government composed of Republican, Peasant, and Communist party representatives. In July, 1946, the Soviets purged the Bulgarian Army, and the leading officers were imprisoned. The Peasant Party, however, commanded considerable support; it had to be destroyed if effective and dependable subservience to Moscow were to be achieved. In 1947 Soviet action against that party was taken: supressing party newspapers, arresting its leaders, and (in September) executing Petkov, the party head, for treason after a "framed" trial. By the end of 1948 the multiparty system had been destroyed. Bulgaria had also joined the ranks of the People's Democracies with an exclusive Communist party political system.

The fate of Poland, Rumania, and Bulgaria also befell Hungary. This country, although occupied by the Soviet army early in 1945, was allowed a relatively free election in November, with the Communists receiving only 17 per cent of the votes. However, a year later in December, 1946, significant interference in the elections took place. Yet even greater interference was called for in 1947 to destroy the Smallholder's Party majority. The Soviet Army moved in with arrests, disenfranchisement of "uncooperative voters," ex post facto disqualification of elected officials, "re-counts," and required acceptance of a Soviet dictated constitution. The Hungarian People's Democracy was proclaimed in 1948.

Soviet Strategy Toward Western Europe

Several tactical changes in Soviet policy toward the West are in evidence during the early postwar years. In 1945–46 it

Joseph Stalin

Joseph Stalin in military uniform during World War II. (Courtesy, Union of Soviet Socialist Republics)

Joseph Stalin was born in a practicing Christian home (Russian Orthodox) and became a student in the Christian theological seminary at Tiflis, the capital city of his native Georgia. Stalin, the man who ruled the Soviet Union for almost thirty years and whose totalitarian rule was characterized as "Ghengis Khan with a telephone," was born on December 21, 1879, as Iosif Vissarionovich Dzhugashvili, in the little village of Gori (close to Tiflis) where his father was a shoemaker. It was only after many aliases to escape the clutches of the Tsar's secret police, that he formally, in 1913, adopted the new name *Stalin* ("man of steel").

His father died in 1891. Two years later his pious, yet illiterate peasant mother found the resources to send him to the Russian Orthodox seminary when "Sosso" (as was his nick name) had not yet reached his fourteenth birthday.

The Russian Tsar was also attempting to use the seminary to preserve the political status quo and promote support for the Tsar's position. The province of Georgia had a reputation for separatist and socialist movements. It was Stalin's involvement in subversive Marxist movements that caused him to be expelled (in 1899) from the seminary shortly before his graduation—a decisive blow to his career as a minister which his mother found disappointing to the end of her life.

He became a member of the inner circle of the Russian Social Democratic Workers party of Tiflis in 1901. A year later he was arrested and eventually sent to Siberia. Escaping in 1904, Stalin returned to Georgia to continue work in the underground Marxist movement which had split (1903) into two groups: a Mensheviks faction advocating a softer strategy of some compromise and evolutionary change, and a Bolsheviks faction taking a much harder line emphasizing the hopelessness of the present order which would have to be destroyed by violence. Stalin sided with the Bolsheviks. The young Marxist from Tiflis met Lenin for the first time at the secret Bolshevik conference at Tammerfors, Finland, in the politically turbulent year of 1905.

Stalin played an important behind-the-scenes role in the success of the Communist revolution in 1917 and in helping the new Soviet regime to survive in the years of the Russian civil war. In 1922 he was elected general secretary of the Communist Party's Central Committee. This put him in a favorable position of patronage and power in the party, which helped him win out over Trotsky in the struggle for power after Lenin's death in 1924.

Stalin's attempt in the 1930s to achieve effective control of the Soviet economy and to deal with the threat from Hitler's Germany turned his ruthless will first against the "obstinate" *kulaks* in 1932–33, when almost 10 million peasants and kulaks were killed by execution and famine. Then in 1937 a bloody purge was launched against the officers of the Soviet Army, and the bureaucracy.

In World War II Stalin achieved Soviet survival by emphasizing "Mother Russia" at the expense of Marxist-Leninist dogma, and by the willingness to trade "space for time" while throwing in more bodies when gaps in the defenses occurred.

After the war Stalin decided to trade a working relationship with the West for his firm control of the vast European territories liberated by his armies.

Senator Claude Pepper (Florida) related an interesting encounter with Stalin. Seven months after the last summit conference during the war against Germany (the Yalta Conference), Senator Pepper visited Moscow. At this time, of the big three at Yalta, only Stalin had survived as a head of state. In a meeting with Stalin in the Kremlin, the Soviet leader lamented to the Senator that the common interest of the wartime coalition against Adolf Hitler was gone. And then, as if thinking aloud, Stalin rhetorically posed the question of how a new basis of cooperation among the former wartime allies could be found. In answering his own question, the former theological seminary student, currently the avowed follower of atheistic Marxist-Leninist thought, quoted Jesus Christ to Senator Pepper in the Biblical quote: "Seek and ye shall find" (Matthew 7, 7; King James Version).

Immediately after World War II Stalin considered expansion in the Middle East as secondary to the goal of furthering Soviet interests in Europe—secondary, that is, except for the border lands of Turkey and Iran, where President Truman's determination to use force in the situation of the American monopoly of atomic weapons made the risks too great.

Stalin was at first in somewhat of a quandary as to diplomatic strategy and tactics in the lower risk Middle East countries beyond the border lands. Finally he made a decision to support the more or less "leftist" oriented Zionists in Palestine in consideration of the fact that this seemed to offer the greatest leverage in getting the British out, since the Arab leadership appeared, at this time, to be hopelessly in collusion with the Western powers entrenched in the Middle East.

Stalin died on March 5, 1953.

---

was generally assumed by Moscow that the United States would be reluctant to use its great potential strength in organizing an anti-Communist coalition against the Soviet Union. The weakness of Britain and France was obvious. Under these circumstances, Stalin decided to have the Communist parties in the more or less democratic states which did not border on the Soviet Union enter national coalitions designed to oppose anti-Soviet policies by mustering veto power from within the structure of party politics.

The basic strategy seems to have been one of presenting a low-threat profile in the Western states of Europe not bordering on the Soviet Union, while gaining effective control of states adjacent to it.

The October, 1945, elections in France gave the participating Communists 25 per cent of the votes; while in November, 1946, elections increased that percentage to 28. The Communist party enjoyed considerable French respect inasmuch as its war record of opposition to German occupation was good. There must have been a temptation for the party to utilize its pinnacle of power to launch an attempt to seize power in Paris, yet orders from Moscow insisted on restraint to coordinate the overall strategy projected by the Soviet Union's leadership. Aggressive political efforts by the French Communists were limited to some minor reshuffling of powers in particular ministries.

The joining of popular government coalitions was also effected by the Italian and the Belgium Communist parties in their respective states at this time. The Soviet affinity toward the socialist orientation of Zionism in Palestine should also be seen in this context of Soviet policy.

The American Response

In 1947 the United States was, however, giving notice of its willingness to act as a leader in organizing a confrontation, if necessary, to stop further Soviet expansion. The United States had already provided, in 1946, a very substantial loan to Britain to boost that country's viability in the face of its deteriorating economy. There was also support for states even more directly threatened by Soviet expansion; the United States responded to the Greek government's request for help on March 3, 1947. Increasing East-West antagonism was proclaimed by Winston Churchill in his famous "Iron Curtain" speech at Westminster College (Fulton, Missouri) in the same month. By June, active support was underway not only for Greece but also for Turkey under the so-called "Truman Doctrine."

A greatly expanded responsibility for the recovery of the war-devastated European economies was called for in General Marshall's Harvard address on June 5, 1947. Invitations were sent to the Soviet Union as well as the states of its east European empire. Czechoslovakia and Poland expressed considerable interest in participating in the American economic program. Yet in the preliminary meeting in Paris, the Russians refused the terms outlined by the United States and later effectively cancelled Poland and Czechoslovakia's interest in participating.

The Marshall Plan involved new calculations of policy for the Soviet Union. Both Britain and France had grave economic weaknesses, and this was becoming increasingly obvious with the passing of time. Soviet aspirations to expand its dominating influence in Europe could only be stopped by a credible threat from the United States. On the one hand, the American monopoly of atomic weapons and, on the other hand, its rapid demobilization right after the war were the parameters of both restraint and opportunity for Soviet policy at this time.

What the Kremlin saw was a new determined American policy to promote economic recovery and military cooperation among the Western democracies in organizing a containment of Soviet aspirations in Europe. Soviet reaction was quick involving changes in three areas.

Soviet Reaction to American Policy

Firstly, orders were sent out from Moscow to the Western Communist parties countermanding their previous directives of 1944–46 in which they had been ordered to support ruling government coalitions. The Communists were now given instructions to organize labor unrest in the service of selected political causes. Strikes, walk-outs, labor demonstrations, etc. represented the new tactics. In France, the Communist members of the Chamber of Deputies voted against the government, which resulted in the dismissal of the Communist cabinet ministers. A major labor strike was called in November, 1947. The Communists had already pulled out of the Italian government in May, 1947. The Belgian Communists had left the Bruxelles government two months before that.

Secondly, there was a renewed emphasis on tightening Moscow's control over the governments of the satellite states and also over the Communist parties in the Western democracies. A new organization for this purpose was created at Wiliza Gora, Poland, in September, 1947, to facilitate this control. Ostensibly, the Cominform, as it was called, was created as a vehicle for exchange of information, but it became evident that the real purpose was to tighten Moscow's control of the Communist parties abroad.

Events stemming from this action were soon visible. In February, 1948, a coup ousted the Czech government which had pushed hard for participation in the Marshall Plan. In the same year the Yugoslav government was expelled from the Cominform for failure to accept a satellite status under Moscow. The Soviet efforts to control the Communist organizations in the Levant, as previously discussed, should be seen in this overall context.

Moscow's renewed attempt at dominating Communist parties abroad did have its impact, as detailed previously, on the Palestine Communist party. Yet it could abandon the party here whenever other, more compelling interests arose (1) because the Soviet Union had only a secondary interest in the Middle East's "southern tier" (Middle East states *not* on its southern border, (2) because the local Communist party seemed hopelessly weak, and (3) because recruitment of rising Arab nationalists had not been successful. One such compelling Soviet interest did develop when the Jews pushed ahead with their objective of freeing themselves from the British Mandatory authority and proclaiming an independent Jewish state in Palestine. By supporting the Jews in this "domestic conflict," the Soviets saw it as an opportunity to get the British out.

The changed Soviet policy toward local Communist parties was unsuccessful in Europe, but the 1949 Communist victory in China encouraged a renewed effort at party domination in other areas of the Far East as exemplified by the later events in Korea, Malaya, etc. The impact of Korea, for instance, escalated the Western containment efforts to build a "northern tier" defense in the Middle East, which in turn helped to create major new antagonisms among Middle East states. These events changed the East-West orientation of the Middle East inasmuch as the post-Stalin era of the Soviet Union sensed new opportunities for a more active involvement in the Middle East. As will be discussed below, this new orientation took an increasingly pro-Arab direction.

Thirdly, in the longer time perspective, there gradually evolved a change in the way the Soviet Union related itself to the third world. This would have a major impact on Soviet policy toward Israel.

Stalin was ideologically attached to the "two camps" concept in foreign policy. This conceptualization of world politics involved the dichotomy of (1) the *socialist camp* (including all those political groups [states] loyal to the Socialist fatherland, the Soviet Union) and (2) the *capitalist–imperialist camp*— untrustworthy, ultimately bourgeois in orientation, and an enemy of the socialist future.

The Stalin regime, therefore, failed to utilize major anti-Western opportunities by failing to support Mossadeq in Iran, 1951–1953, and Nasser in Egypt immediately after the 1952 coup. Both were dismissed as essentially untrustworthy in successfully dealing with the imperialism of bourgeois Britain (and the Western states in general). Stalin's tendency to dismiss third world states as "capitalist controlled" reduced the potential of Soviet foreign policy to exploit the opportunities in the post-war disintegration of the Western empires.

Soviet Domestic Politics

After Stalin died on March 5, 1953, the "two camps" categorization of international politics was no longer emphasized. Instead, Stalin's successors moved toward a new conceptualization of exploitation and the exploited. At the Twentieth Congress of the Soviet Communist Party, February, 1956, Khrushchev first used the image of "two zones;" the "peace zone" now included not only the socialist states attached to the authentic leadership of Moscow, but also the non-socialist states of the Afro-Asian world whose native nationalists were seeking to throw off the yoke of Western imperialism. This made it possible to formulate a whole new ideological approach toward the states of Africa and Asia.

Stalin's successor, Malenkov, presented India and Burma in a favorable context for the first time only five months after the death of Stalin. A month later, Moscow signed a five-year trade agreement with India. Within two years the Soviets had given very substantial support to the Bandung Conference (April, 1955) which catapulted Nasser to stardom in the Arab Middle East. In mid-November, 1955, Bulganin and Khrushchev made their well-publicized visit to India (as well as visits to Burma and Afghanistan). In the same year, the Soviets exploded on the Middle East scene through the negotiated arms deal with Egypt, breaking the Western arms embargo set up by Britain, France and the United States in the Tripartite Declaration of May, 1950.

Although these events will be explored later, suffice it here to note the increasingly pro-Arab position of the Soviet Union after Stalin's death. It was based upon the official policy line that the third world was moving in the direction of national socialism and anti-imperialism. Because these goals were "in the right direction," the Soviet Union should undertake to promote and encourage this commonality by a pro-Arab policy. Much greater confidence was now officially placed in the "national bourgeoisie." They were now seen as working toward the cause of national independence rather than betraying the aspirations of the masses by simply exchanging one form of exploitation, under *overt* dependence on the capitalist West, for another exploitive situation under the *facade* of independence.

In analyzing the radical Soviet switch from pro-Israel to

'ALWAYS HAPPY TO HELP A PAL'

After the death of Stalin the Soviet Union became aware of the potential advantages in fanning the flames of nationalism in the Middle East. (Bimrose in The Portland Oregonian)

pro-Arab, one notes how Soviet decision-making, like political decision-making elsewhere, is done in an arena of competition among mutually exclusive alternatives—competing alternatives with their respective advocates among the decision-making elite. In 1948, for instance, in the Zhdanov-Malenkov clash, the former argued for a militant, aggressive posture in foreign policy versus the latter's insistence upon a more inward-oriented, "Russia first" policy. But even more importantly, the rivalry between Malenkov and Khrushchev after Stalin's death resulted in the former's ouster on February 8, 1955.

The "Right" and the "Left" in Soviet Politics

In broad generalizations, it is useful to look at Soviet domestic politics in terms of political strategies of *the right* and of *the left*. On the *left* the emphasis is upon the immediate revolutionary act, upon "transformation," "mobilization," the use of violence (if necessary), discontinuity in history, the priority of ideological demands, the inevitability of war with the capitalist camp, support for heavy industry, etc. In contrast, the Communist *right* looks upon successful policy as requiring "some adjustment," "stabilization," "normalization," relatively greater concern for Soviet national interests (than that of Communist ideology when significant costs and risks are involved), detente, emphasis upon consumer goods, etc. More simply expressed, the left versus the Communist right can be characterized as "the Red versus the expert" or "warfare Communism" versus "welfare Communism."

The switch from a pro-Israel to a pro-Arab policy should, therefore, also be seen in the context of Kremlin leadership rivalry in which those who emphasized the leftist-socialist views of the Jewish pioneer settlements in Palestine were closer to Soviet ideology than those who wanted to support the Arab side with its conservative Islamic identity. Yet the switch toward the Arab side, rationalized in the *two zones* conceptualization of international politics, served in this situation as the arena of combat for leadership rivalry as it evolved in the Kremlin.

Alternatively, if analyzed substantively rather than as inter-party strife, the *two zones* conceptualization did represent a more pragmatic, national interest strategy for the Soviet Union to gain at U.S. expense in the cold war. Soviet national interests had an opportunity resulting from the U. S. ideological attachment to Israel; Americans emotionally favored the Jewish state.

Khrushchev Takes Over

Khrushchev ultimately won out in the leadership struggle. Through his initiative, the *two camps* official analysis of the world community ("the good guys" versus "the bad guys") was modified by the *two zones* conceptualization. The capitalist–imperialist West made up the *war zone*. Now, however, the *peace zone* included not only the states of the Socialist fatherland, but also the anti-colonial, "peace-loving" states of the colonial and post-colonial world. This provided a rationalization for Soviet Communist ideology when it became clear to Khrushchev that Soviet national interests could be promoted by replacing a "vinegar" policy with a "sugar" policy toward the third world.

This new conceptualization of the peace zone versus the war zone made it possible, for instance, to transfer Gamal Abdul Nasser from the "bourgeois nationalist" category of the anti-Socialist camp to the "zone of peace" which included the Soviet Union. While this particular solution to the problem was new, the problem itself was not. Lenin had struggled with the issue and suggested that oppressed states had a contribution to make in the worldwide Socialist revolution. In these colonial or exploited states which had no significant proletarian class, a local nationalist army which was "progressive" in ideology might be the initial vanguard in leading the country toward authentic Socialism—particularly would this be true where the military officers could trace their roots to having come from the "working class."[2]

This Soviet sophistry created some problems in Syria, however, where the leading self-proclaimed Communist of the Arab world, Khalid Bakdash, (for reasons of obvious vested interests) was not happy with the generosity of the Soviet theoreticians in giving "vanguard" status to "officer patriots" in the "transition of a national liberation movement to Communism."[3]

Nikita Khrushchev

Premier Nikita S. Khrushchev at the United Nations, October, 1960. (Courtesy, The United Nations)

Although Nikita Khrushchev spent many years working and promoting the Soviet Communist party in the Ukraine, he was not born in the Ukraine. His place of birth was the village of Kalinovka near the city of Kursk where his father was a miner. Born on April 17, 1894, he became a mechanic's apprentice in his youth, working on the mining equipment and machinery of the coke plant. He was drafted into the Russian army when Nicholas II took Russia into World War I. In the disastrous year of the Brest-Litovsk Treaty (1918), Nikita Khrushchev joined the Communist party. He then fought on the side of the Reds in the Russian civil war.

After the civil war he went back to work in the mines of the Ukraine. He was now in his late twenties and had very little formal schooling. A party sponsored technical high school, the Donets Industrial Institute, became available to him at this time; he seized the opportunity, graduating in 1925.

Khrushchev was now ready to devote his life to the Communist party. He began his career as a full-time party official in 1925, becoming district party secretary in the coal mining center of Stalino in the Ukraine. Later he was transferred to the capital city of the Ukraine, Kiev.

In 1929, the extrovert, aggressive, second generation party worker was transferred to Moscow to attend the Industrial Academy for training in industrial administration. While in school he became secretary of the academy's party committee. Upon graduation in 1931 he became a district party secretary in Moscow and utilized his new expertise in public administration to help build the famous Moscow subway, for which he received the Order of Lenin award.

Nikita Khrushchev broke into the ranks of top party officialdom with his election to the Central Committee of the Soviet Union in 1934, being promoted, in 1935, to First Secretary of the Moscow Regional Committee.

He escaped from Stalin's wrath in the party purges. A series of transfers and promotions followed which included work as First Secretary of the Communist party of the Ukraine and various responsibilities in the Red Army during World War II. After Stalin died on

March 5, 1953, he edged himself into the position of First Secretary of the Communist party's Central Committee—receiving the formal designation of this position in September, 1953. This placed him in a powerful position to compete in the top leadership struggle for succession to Stalin's dominant role in the Soviet Union. In this struggle, Khrushchev vanquished Beria, Malenkov, Molotov, and finally Bulganin to become, in 1955, the dominant political leader of the Soviet Union. In 1958 he received the formal title of Chairman of the Council of Ministers (Prime Minister), which made him officially the head of government in addition to his head of party role as First Secretary of the Communist party's Central Committee.

Khrushchev's domestic program emphasized the development of Soviet agriculture. In foreign policy he pushed for a recognition of the status quo in Europe. With the European front stabilized by a tacit status quo understanding with the West, he saw new opportunities for expansion of Soviet influence in the Middle East and South Asia (eventually Castro's Cuba was successfully added to these aspirations).

It was in relation to the Middle East that Khrushchev's greatest departure from Stalin's third world policies occurred. Stalin had used a *two-camps* ideological model which discounted the anti-Western nationalism in the Afro-Asian world of Western colonialism. There was the *socialist camp* composed of all states loyal to Moscow. In the other camp—the *capitalist-imperialist camp*—were the enemies of the socialist states, and this category included not only the Western states, but also the third world states which had not yet come under Moscow's irreversible leadership. To Stalin, the local nationalists like Nasser, Mossadeq, Nehru, etc. were still enemies of the socialist camp, fickle and unreliable as allies in the international class war.

On the other hand, Nikita Khrushchev saw possibilities for the Soviet Union in supporting anti-

Western nationalists in the third world, and he presented a new *two-zone* ideological model to replace the two camps conceptualization of Stalin. The "peace zone" was now enlarged to include not only the socialist states attached to Moscow, but also those areas of the Afro-Asian world whose native nationalists were effectively involved in throwing off the yoke of Western imperialism.

Khrushchev, nevertheless, did make a special effort to recreate "solidarity" in the configuration of Moscow-dominated socialist states. He spent considerable effort to repair the cracks in relations with Yugoslavia and China.

Major policy confrontations included Khrushchev's de-Stalinization bombshell at the Twentieth Congress of the Communist Party (1956), and the threat of war with the United States in the Cuban missile crisis of 1962. Somewhat less serious was the confrontation in the 1956 tripartite invasion of Egypt.

Khrushchev also had failures, and his unilateral, bombastic style of leadership developed jealousies and apprehension. While on business away from Moscow, the party leaders met and voted his ouster from power in October, 1964. He died on September 11, 1971.

NOTES

1. David J. Dallin, *Soviet Foreign Policy After Stalin* (New York: Lippincott Co., 1961), p. 109.

2. Jean Pennar, "The Soviet Road to Damascus," *Mizan* 9 (January–February 1967): 26.

3. Ibid., p. 28.

Part II:

The Pro-Arab Period

CHAPTER 6

Initial Stress in Relations with Israel: Jews in the Soviet Union

As time passed, the USSR soon realized the potential of harnessing Arab antagonism against the West to use for its own benefit. Yet the potential could be effectively realized only if the Soviet Union turned against Israel. The very act of abandoning Israel would in itself "deposit Arab goodwill in the Soviet account" which could be drawn upon as required by the Kremlin's cold war policy.

This Soviet potential for Arab goodwill was a result of American emotional attachment to Israel and the continued British military presence in Egypt, and to a lesser degree in both Jordan and Iraq. Arab nationalists saw the issue as Western colonialism.

To the delight of the Arabs, the original circumstances of Soviet support for Israel were now changing. These original circumstances could be summarized as follows:

(1) There was the perceived opportunity to reduce British influence in the Middle East.

(2) Arab national movements had developed enthusiasm for fascism in the late 1930s and during World War II.

(3) The Soviet government had discounted the importance of the Arab Middle East to its post-war national interests. (Some political analysts have suggested that Stalin approved the pro-Israel policy, which was recommended by subordinates, in a moment of carelessness or lethargy.)

(4) The Arab leadership was considered hopelessly reac-

tionary and in collusion with British imperialism against the masses. Great Britain's efforts in the creation of the Arab League were seen as an attempt by the British to maintain their imperialist grip over the Arab Middle East. The Arab leaders had been willing subjects in this ploy.

(5) Many of Israel's leaders were immigrants from Russia and had roots in socialist causes there. A bond of friendship had been nurtured in common hatred of the Nazis during World War II. Moscow was hopeful that it might be possible to use Israel for support in its foreign policy objectives.

(6) Even beyond an ideological bond, the Soviet Union was interested in being repaid for its crucial support in Israel's creation. As related by Schweitzer:

> The Soviet Union hoped that the gratitude of the Jews in Israel for Soviet support would find expression in a pro-Soviet policy on the part of the Israeli government. The pro-Soviet element was indeed not to be disregarded in the new state. It included the United Labour Party (Mapam), the Israeli Communist Party (Maki) and many sympathizers among the Israeli population.[1]

In any case, thanks to the Soviet Union (and other states), the United Nations gave Israel a legal basis for its creation. Its *de facto* existence was, nevertheless, achieved by the Israelis themselves in militarily defeating the Arab states' military invasion. Yet in the war itself, Israel was helped along by the Soviet decision to sell arms to hard-pressed Israeli military forces. As discussed, the first Czech arms (arranged with the Soviet Union) reached the Yishuv in March, 1948, almost two months before the proclamation of the state of Israel.[2] During the course of the war, Israel was dependent upon these arms from eastern Europe plus whatever could be stolen from the British army.[3] In contrast, the Arabs fought with arms supplied by the British.[4] Official United States policy was to embargo the shipment of arms to both sides (although Israel scored a few successes in dodging the FBI and smuggling material out of the United States[5]).

Golda Meir in Moscow

After the war which made the existence of Israel a fact of international life, the course of events started a slow cooling of relations between Israel and the USSR. In tracing the change, one begins with the otherwise innocent event of Golda Myerson's[6] (Meir) arrival in Moscow on September 6, 1948, to be Israel's first Minister to the Soviet Union.

Having left Russia at age eight under circumstances of threatened pogroms in 1906, she had both a personal as well as an official interest in getting information about the state of the Soviet Jews. On the day after the presentation of her credentials (Saturday, September 11), members of the Israeli legation attended services at the main synagogue in Moscow. At the close of the service it was customary for the Rabbi to say a blessing for the Soviet head of state. But on this Saturday the Rabbi also asked the blessing for Golda Meir—an act which served to inform the 100 or more worshippers that the representative of the new Zionist state of Israel was in their midst. That meeting sparked an emotional response for Israel in the Moscow Jewish community.

Mrs. Meir raised the issue of Jewish immigration to Israel in her first meeting with the head of the Middle Eastern Department of the Soviet Foreign Ministry. On September 16 the Soviet government received its first applications from Soviet Jews requesting permission to immigrate to Israel.[7] The Soviet leaders were thrown on the defensive by the unexpected wave of pro-Israel sentiment which now arose in Moscow.

The outpouring of emotion for Jews of the new state of Israel climaxed at the celebration of the Jewish New Year (Rosh Hashanah) on October 6. Even beyond Golda Meir's wildest expectations, the street in front of the synagogue "was filled with people, packed together like sardines, hundreds and hundreds of them, of all ages, including Red Army officers, soldiers, teenagers, and babies carried in their parents' arms."[8] The normal attendance at the synagogue on major

Jewish holidays was approximately 2,000. In contrast, on this occasion there were an estimated 50,000 waiting to catch a glimpse of Israel's first Head of Mission in Moscow. They had come "to demonstrate their sense of kinship and to celebrate the establishment of" the State of Israel. Mrs. Meir relates how the occasion almost became a riot when the human wave pressed close to her to touch her hand or to kiss her dress.

Golda Meir was the symbol of the new Jewish state in Palestine, and somehow it became an irresistible attraction to the Russian Jews to use the occasion in celebration of Israel's creation.[9]

Soviets Crush Spark of Zionism in Russia

The wave of emotion for Israel caught the authorities off guard. These events were observed by the Soviet government with a great amount of displeasure. After 30 years, to have this kind of Jewish identity ready to explode on the scene by the mere visit of a foreign dignitary was cause for alarm. The historical experience of the Jews in the Soviet Union had been one of a certain amount of regime intimidation to avoid an unnecessary amount of direct application of state power. But many Soviet Jews assumed that some identification with the new state of Israel would be acceptable behavior in view of the Soviet Union's overt support for the creation of Israel. Earlier, some Jews had been even naive enough to petition the government for permission to use their individual military skills to fight with the hard-pressed Jewish forces in the first Arab-Israeli war. It was obvious that the Soviets were very sensitive about the various nationality groups within the Soviet Union identifying with a foreign state. Jews were especially watched. Not only did it elicit a concern in the traditional sense of possible disloyalty to the state and the "fifth column" danger in international crises, it was also an affront to Communist ideology to have native groups appear unconvinced of the glories of the superior Communist society achieved in the Soviet Union.

The government's apprehension had already been expressed a few days before the Rosh Hashanah events when the state had instituted the publication of an article in *Pravda*[10] by the Soviet apologist, Ilya Ehrenberg (a Jew), to remind the Jews that it was Stalin whose crucial influence had been responsible for the creation of Israel. Nevertheless, wrote Ehrenberg, Israel is no concern of the Soviet Jews who have all been effectively integrated into the Communist society and who have experienced the happiness of the great social achievements of the Soviet Union. There is no longer a Jewish nationality because the Jews have assimilated in the Socialist fatherland.

All Zionist activity and the study of Hebrew were categorized by the Communist regime as "bourgeois deviations" and banned in 1919 (although some Jewish calendars and a few religious books were still published until 1928). The reason for this was that immediately after the Communist revolution in 1917 there was an attempt to "bend" Judaism and the Jewish culture to conform to the state policy of Communist ideology. At that time the Soviet Communist party organized, from its Jewish members, "Jewish Sections" called Yevsektsiya. These Yevsektsiya were given the responsibility of imposing " 'the proletarian dictatorship among the Jewish masses.' "[11] The new Bolshevik regime of Russia was initially required to recognize the millions of Russian Jews as a fact of life. Thus the Yevsektsiya embarked upon an opportunist strategy of accepting a secular Jewish culture (via the vehicle of the Yiddish language) to get rid of Judaism and the national organization of Jews in Russia. It was also a matter of expediency in view of the precarious status at that time of the Communist regime, both as the government of Russia domestically, and as a *de facto* actor internationally. Thus "Jewish proletarian culture" was to replace Judaism as a matter of expediency in the initial era of Communism in Russia.

When the new Bolshevik government took over, it also incorporated in its official government machinery a Jewish commissariat to deal with the Jews. While the Soviet government's treatment of Jews prior to 1948 was quite similar to that given other ethnic (national) minorities, during the later years of Stalin's rule, anti-Jewish government actions tended to exclude them from the status of an officially recognized minority.[12] They were still registered as Jews, but government policy took away from them the rights of cultural expression which other national minorities had. Yiddish schools, newspapers, periodicals, theatres, etc. became a thing of the past.[13]

The greater Soviet apprehension about the growth of a Jewish identity (especially after the creation of Israel) had several roots: (1) Jews in the Soviet Union had many relatives in other countries. These links, it was felt, could create security problems for the USSR. (2) Jews performed many highly skilled and vital roles for the Soviet economy and for the development of military weapons. (3) They were also widely scattered geographically, which made surveillance of them more difficult relative to national groups which were concentrated in a single geographical area; if not detected early by internal security forces, a dissident movement in the cosmopolitan centers of the large cities would be a much more formidable threat to the regime than a geographically isolated one. (4) Judaism had a highly developed value system which differed from the official Communist party ideology. As a result of all of these factors, the Jews suffered the liabilities of having to register as a minority, yet were barred from the benefits of that designation in terms of enjoying the cultural institutions of their national identity. In summary, a government policy of complete assimilation (no Jewish identity) would make it difficult to apprehend Jewish clandestine oppositional movements.

To return to the events of late 1948 and Golda Meir's spark of Jewish nationalism as a result of the Rosh Hashanah events in the Soviet Union, the Soviet authorities moved in to curtail this kind of Jewish behavior. The Soviets let it be known that such Jewish activity was "inadvisable." After October, the Jewish mass enthusiasm for contacts with Israel's officialdom tended to disappear. Many leading Jews who were considered

leaders in the cultural or religious expression of Jewish identity "were imprisoned, deported, and executed."[14] Not all of
the government's action stemmed specifically from the Rosh
Hashanah events. The Soviet Union had already begun an
anti-Jewish campaign earlier—in late 1947 extending into
1948. These government measures against Jews in the USSR
seem to have been unrelated to what the Jews in Palestine,
and later Israel, were doing. However, after Golda Meir arrived in Moscow in September, the Rosh Hashanah and other
events involving the Israeli representatives did have an increased impact. In the last three months of 1948 the Jewish
Anti-Fascist Committee was eliminated. The publication,
Anynikayt, was shut down, as was the Der Emes publishing
house. Finally, the last two important Jewish cultural
institutions—the Jewish library and the Yiddish Theater (both
in Moscow) were closed down in November, 1949.[15] There is
evidence to indicate that several thousand Jewish families
from the Ukraine were forced to leave their homes to be trans-
ported to the harsh existence in Biro-Bidjan.[16]

But the events of a Jewish awakening in Russia, triggered
by the new Israeli Minister in Moscow, were not over. On
November 7, 1948, Foreign Minister Viacheslav Molotov held
a large reception in his home in honor of the Soviet Revolution. Mrs. Molotov made a special effort to meet Golda Meir.
The latter relates the meeting as follows:

> . . . Ivy Molotov . . . came up to me. "I am so pleased to meet
> you, at last," she said with real warmth and even excitement.
> Then she added: "I speak Yiddish, you know."
> "Are you Jewish?" I asked in some surprise.
> "Yes," she said, answering me in Yiddish, "I am a daughter of
> the Jewish people."
> We talked together for quite a long time. She knew all about
> the events at the synagogue and told me how good it was that we
> had gone. "The Jews wanted so much to see you," she said.[17]

Mrs. Molotov insisted on meeting Golda Meir's daughter,
Sarah, and Yael Namir, the 15-year-old daughter of Mordekhai

Namir, Israeli Counselor at the legation. The wife of the Soviet official was particularly interested in questioning Sarah about her life in the Revvim Kibbutz (in the Negev)—all in Yiddish. According to Golda Meir:

> Before she [Ivy Molotov] returned to her other guests, she put her arm around Sarah and, with tears in her eyes said: "Be well. If everything goes well with you, it will go well for all Jews everywhere."[18]

Mrs. Molotov's enthusiasm for Jewish culture and the new state of Israel was catching. Diplomats from the various Soviet satellite states now participated in the new subject of conversation. A number of these diplomats mentioned the fact that their wives were Jews.

Shortly after this meeting, Mrs. Molotov was arrested and sent into exile. Her pro-Jewish enthusiasm had exceeded the bounds of tolerance allowed by Soviet officialdom.

Golda Meir concludes her observation about the Jews in Russia by noting that:

> ... By January 1949 it was apparent that Russian Jewry was going to pay a heavy price for the welcome it had given us, for the "treachery to Communist Ideals" that was—in the eyes of the Soviet government—implicit in the joy with which we had been greeted.[19]

The Soviet government now took steps to halt any future demonstrations of Jewish attraction to members of the Israeli diplomatic mission in Moscow. As already mentioned, the Yiddish publishing house in Moscow, Emes, was forced to cease operations. *Enigkeit*, the Yiddish newspaper, was shut down and the Yiddish theatre, which had at one time achieved considerable prestige as an art form, was closed.[20]

The chain of events reflected the sensitivities of both the Soviet Union and Israel to Soviet Jewry. Both had special interests at stake—interests so important that it is easy for outside observers to misunderstand the seemingly excessive reactions of each side to the situation. At the heart of Zionism is the belief in the importance of a Jewish state to act as the protector for all Jews who have, since the Diaspora, continuously experienced the humiliation of anti-semitism and even physical abuse—occasionally touching on genocide.

The Soviets, for both ideological reasons and because of perceived threats to their national territorial integrity, have been very apprehensive of Jewish nationalism and, in these circumstances, Jewish contacts with foreign states. In the events of 1948, the Soviet Union was in no mood to accept Israel's interference in its internal affairs. On the other hand, Israel was under pressure from its own domestic citizenry to establish contacts with Soviet Jews and to work for emancipation from the restraints on their existence as Jews. The most satisfactory solution, in popular opinion, was (and still is) immigration to Israel.

NOTES

1. Karmi Shweitzer, "Soviet Policy Towards Israel 1946–1952," *Mizan* 11 (January–February 1969): 21.

2. Yaacov Ro'i, "The Soviet Union, Israel and the Arab-Israel Conflict," *The U.S.S.R. and the Middle East*, eds. Michael Confino and Shimon Shamir (Jerusalem: Israel University Press, 1973), p. 128.

3. Some World War II weapons from western Europe and the United States also found their way into Israel.

4. Ro'i, p. 128.

5. See Benjamin Kagan, *The Secret Battle for Israel* (Cleveland: World Publishing Co., 1966).

6. Golda Myerson Hebraized her name to Meir in July, 1956.

7. Avigdor Dagan, *Moscow and Jerusalem* (New York: Abelard–Schuman, 1970), p. 37.

8. Golda Meir, *My Life* (London: Weidenfeld and Nicolson, 1975), p. 205.

9. Ibid., pp. 205–206.

10. *Pravda*, Sept. 21, 1948.

11. "Russia," *Encyclopedia Judaica*, 1971, XIV: 464.

12. Ro'i, p. 130.

13. Ben Ami, *Between Hammer and Sickle* (Philadelphia: The Jewish Publication Society of America, 1967), p. 24.

14. Ro'i, p. 130.

15. Ibid., p. 143.

16. Dagan, p. 46.

17. Meir, p. 208.

18. Ibid.

19. Ibid., p. 209.

20. Ibid.

CHAPTER 7

Moscow Accuses Israel of Leaning Toward the West

For the first time, in late 1948, the Soviet press came out with criticism of the "anti-Soviet" attitude in Israel—an ungrateful attitude for the support the USSR had given Israel at its creation. The Soviet Union in late 1948 also became concerned lest Israel, after asserting its effective independence from Britain, would compromise its sovereignty to United States influence. Professor V. B. Lutskii, a Russian Middle East expert, mentioned in a public lecture in Moscow the Soviet concern that Israel might become an American protectorate.[1] Sensing the increased Soviet apprehensions about Israel swinging toward the West in the rising East-West tensions, Mrs. Meir had a meeting with Soviet Foreign Minister Andrei Vyshinsky before her return to Israel on April 20, 1949 (to become Minister of Labor in Ben Gurion's government). Earlier in February, the Soviet press had carried reports of a Western move to establish a pro-West military alliance in the Middle East together with the rumor that Israel would join. Ambassador Panyushkin of the Soviet Embassy in Washington inquired of the Israeli ambassador whether this was true. At the time Panyushkin simply cautioned Israel by noting that he was not asking Israel to join the Soviet aligned states, but he felt Israel should also refrain from joining a Western alliance.[2] Now, when Mrs. Meir made the farewell visit to Vyshinsky, she felt it advisable to calm Moscow's apprehensions about this matter. Meir's reaffirmation of Israel's policy to remain neutral in the East-West confrontation seemed to have been taken in good faith at this time (April 16, 1949).[3]

Yet the concern was not permanently laid to rest. Moscow assumed that its original support for the creation of Israel had established Israeli political indebtedness which could be "cashed in" as time passed. Hence, Moscow questioned whether the American Export-Import Bank loan to Israel in February, 1949, would also lead to financial obligations to be paid for in pro-American political ties. On March 20 a Soviet correspondent had cabled Moscow from Tel Aviv quoting MAKI (The Israeli Communist Party) as stating that the American loan was leading to U.S. economic controls over Israel.[4] Deputy Foreign Minister Zorin questioned Mordekhai Namir[5] of the Israeli legation about this on May 5. Namir replied that Israel was a sovereign state and would never permit its sovereignty to be compromised. Furthermore, Israel was interested in treating both sides equally and was, therefore, willing also to receive financial aid from the USSR.

At this time, obviously, no peace treaties with the Arab states had yet been signed; Syria had not even agreed to an armistice. Israel was still very much concerned about its survival. Namir expressed appreciation for the Soviet Union's diplomatic support. Zorin responded by saying that Soviet support would continue as long as Israel continued "'on the right political line.'"[6] Presumably this meant that Israel should refrain from adopting a pro-United States policy.

To counteract this impression that Israel was following a pro-Western policy, Moshe Sharett, the Israeli Foreign Minister, decided in June, 1949, to invite Gromyko to Israel, hoping that the visit would serve as a proof of Israel's neutrality since the visit would not be to Western liking. In October, 1949, Namir denied reports reaching the Soviet government that the Israeli Army would be organized on the American pattern.[7]

Moscow was apparently satisfied with Israel's policy between East and West during the Security Council debate on the admission of Israel to United Nations membership. Thus in May, 1949, when Israel became the 59th member of the United Nations, Moscow was still giving Israel diplomatic support in international affairs, yet a qualifying danger signal

appeared in the Polish delegate's speech (which was generally assumed to be the mouthpiece of the Soviet bloc at this
time). The warning to Israel was clear as emphasized in the
following record of his speech:

> The period of sentimental interest in the fate of Israel has come to
> an end; an era of cooperation based on mutual interest is begin-
> ning. The Jewish people, advancing along peaceful and progres-
> sive lines, could rely on the assistance of Poland, the Soviet Re-
> publics and the People's Democracies of Europe. Israel will
> doubtless remember that those countries had been its true friends
> at the troubled time of its emergence. It was not long since the
> British Foreign Office had tried and failed to prevent the creation
> of Israel. United Kingdom and the United States diplomacy had
> been ready to betray the new State before its birth. The United
> States Government's change of policy with regard to Israel had
> occurred for reasons of political expediency divorced from any
> sense of justice or faith in Israel's future. That should not be
> forgotten. . . . Neither should it be forgotten that Israel was deeply
> indebted to the working classes. Poland will watch the future of
> Israel with sympathetic interest.[8]

The implications were clear; the Soviet Union was advis-
ing Israel to be on the Soviet side of the East-West ideological
conflict and to refrain from supporting pro-Western policy in
international politics. Israel must understand that "IOU's" are
to be honored if it wished further diplomatic support.

Additional evidence of Soviet concern for "proper" Israeli
behavior can be seen from such semi-official criticism as that
expressed, for instance, by Soviet orientalist, Vladimir Lutskii,
in Moscow, June, 1949, in a paper at the symposium sponsored jointly by the Pacific Institute of the Academy of Sciences and the Institute of Economics. Lutskii, at this time,
maintained

> that Israel had not fulfilled the conditions imposed on the Jewish
> state [by the United Nations]. The partition resolution of
> November 1947 . . . had called for "the establishment of an inde-

pendent, democratic Jewish state." Yet Israel was being built up as "a Zionist bourgeois state." She opened her gates to foreign capital, accepted a loan from the Export-Import Bank on conditions inconsistent with state sovereignty, and expressed her readiness "to join the aggressive Mediterranean bloc knocked together by the Anglo-American imperialists." Israel's leaders . . . opposed the World Peace Congress (held April 1949), demanded that Israel trade unions leave the World Federation of Trade Unions, and were truckling to the Anglo-American bloc at the United Nations.[9]

Lutskii, a loyal Soviet, anti-Zionist Jew, continued by justifying the USSR's support for the creation of Israel and its supplying of arms to Israel in the 1948 war against the Arab states:

"The Palestine war . . . sharpened the crisis of the colonial system in the Near East, demonstrated to the Arab popular masses all the rottenness and the reactionary nature of the ruling cliques of the Arab countries, and exposed their intimate ties with English and American imperialism."[10]

Lutskii, however, concluded with an implicit warning to Israel. The objective conditions for national liberation movements among the Arab masses were coming into being. The implication being that Soviet support for liberation movements among the Arabs might warrant future considerations.

In addition to these developments of 1949, conflicting situations also arose in Israel's relations with the Soviet satellite states of eastern Europe over the domestic treatment of Jews and their right to emigrate. For example, the Israeli Minister Reuven Rubin was recalled from Bucharest because Rumania refused to allow Rumanian Jews to immigrate to Israel. This indicated the significance Israel attached to the right of Jews to return to their ancestral home.[11]

The clash of Israeli–Soviet interests over the treatment of Soviet Jews and the denial of Jewish immigration to Israel has already been discussed. Yet in spite of difficulties related to this issue, Moscow continued a basic pro-Israel, anti-Arab policy throughout 1949. As late as December 9 Soviet spokesman Tsarapkin was still publicly referring to King Abdullah of Jordan as a "'British puppet and an obedient henchman of United Kingdom policy in the Middle East....' "[12] The Soviets tended to view Egypt as similarly under British imperial control. As a matter of fact, they had always considered the Arab League as a tool of British imperialism.

USSR Sensitive to Israel's Pro-Western Potential

Although Israel occasionally found itself on the side of the West on UN issues as they arose in late 1949, the issues were relatively unimportant for the USSR and, furthermore, the Arab states were even more consistently against the Soviet bloc in UN votes, so the enticement to switch clients in the Middle East was not in evidence. Note, for example, the Israeli vote on the General Assembly resolution of December 1, 1949, condemning the preparation of states for a new war. Israel supported the United States position against the Soviet proposal. Tsarapkin, of the Soviet Union, called the Israeli delegate's attention to this "anti-Soviet attitude." Yet, with all the Arab members of the United Nations (except Yemen) also casting their votes against the Soviet proposed resolution, Tsarapkin had no readily available threat to keep Israel in line. This situation would change as a new generation of nationalist leaders arose who would have no qualms against playing one side off against the other for their own national interests.

Already in April, 1949, Sulzberger's analysis, in *The New York Times*, of the future Israeli–Soviet relations turned out to be prophetic. Said Sulzberger, Moscow was shrewd enough to know by now that its hope of gaining a foothold in the Middle East via Israel was unrealistic. On the one hand, Israel's foreign policy had gravitated farther from the Soviet orbit as the West became more attractive in terms of economic aid and basic political values. On the other hand, Israel would not be dissuaded from requesting the right of Jews to leave Soviet dominated eastern Europe. The logical outcome would be for the Soviets to explore the anti-Western potential of the frustrated and defeated Arabs.[13] The year 1950 was, however, a year of vacillation.

In January, 1950, the Communist press began to attack Israeli leaders on a broad front of issues. The American Secretary of the Treasury's visit to Israel was criticized for seeking to enlist Israel in the capitalist encirclement of the Soviet fatherland. Criticism was also expressed for what was felt to be the threat of Israel joining a rumored Western-Middle East military alliance against the Soviet Union. This thread of events will be picked up again later.

Nevertheless, at this time the Soviets did not entirely alienate the Israeli government. Moscow considered Israel to be the strongest military power in the area and, in a communication to the latter, implied an appreciation of its neutrality in the East-West conflict. This was in contrast to the Soviet's characterization of Egypt, Iraq, and Syria as being bases of aggression. Even as late as mid-June, the Soviet government reassured Israel of its strong support in the Jerusalem question.

In 1950 there were, however, two major events which contributed to a serious deterioration of Soviet-Israeli relations. These were (1) the Tripartite Declaration of May 25 and (2) the Korean War which erupted on June 25.

Before discussing these two important developments, let us recall the broad context of Soviet policy toward the Middle East in general. Immediately after World War II the Soviets adopted a strong Middle East policy, focusing on realizing objectives against Greece, Turkey, and Iran. By late 1948 this thrust into the Middle East had waned in failure. It led to a general disenchantment with the Middle East as an opportunity for Soviet efforts. To be sure, its support for the creation of Israel was successful, but the independence of Israel had worked no miracle for increased Soviet influence in the Mid-

'COMING TO A BOIL'

Carmack, in The Christian Science Monitor, *depicts the oil fired pot of Middle East politics "coming to a boil." The Soviet Union is on the horizon and beginning to take an increasing interest in the heat of political passions in that area of the world.*

dle East. As a result Moscow reduced its expectations and its efforts in the area. The Soviet Union had no strong Communist party in the Arab world and, in the absence of a significant nationalistic revolutionary movement in the Middle East, there was an ebb of significant Soviet foreign policy interest in relation to this part of the world. Success in Soviet-led expansion of Communism after World War II had been a function of the Soviet military forces "liberating" its European borderlands in World War II. Stalin's sense of political realism made him aware of the importance of military occupation to achieve successful political domination. Indeed, perhaps he was overly awed by the military dimension, for Soviet policy failed to take advantage of the 1951–52 Middle East opportunities in the Mossadeq upheavals of Iran and the "Black Saturday" turmoil in Egypt—both occurring after the Tripartite Declaration and the outbreak of the Korean War. The outbreak of the Korean War created a sense of renewed urgency among the Western powers for the building of a containment alliance in the Middle East. Alternatively, the Soviet Union looked upon the proposed Western alliance as a new threat to its national interests.

West Recognizes Potential for Soviet Expansion in Middle East

It should also be noted that the waning of Soviet involvement in the Middle East for a few years after 1948 created a favorable anti-colonial image of the USSR in Arab eyes. The Soviets' lack of Middle East involvement at this time produced a relatively innocent image of the USSR in contrast to the West in the decolonization struggle. This proved to be an asset which the Soviets were able to draw upon in the East–West rivalry for the region in the later 1950s.

After the creation of Israel with strong Soviet support, knowledgeable Western officials believed that it would only be a matter of time before a new thrust of traditional Russian

In summer, 1950, the United States viewed with considerable alarm the Soviet support of North Korean Aggression. The U.S. believed the attack might well represent a new Soviet policy of willingness to use military force in the cold war confrontation. Unrest in Iran occurred in spring, 1951, when the Iranian Majlis voted to nationalize the British-owned oil company in Iran. Soviet involvement in these events was not immediately clear, but the cartoon conjectured a possible Soviet challenge in the oil fields of Iran as a new thrust subsequent to catching the West off guard in Korea. (Reprinted with permission from The Nashville Tennessean)

expansion into the Middle East could be expected. The rising East-West confrontation known as the "cold war," plus the increasing restiveness of Egypt over the presence of the large

British military base at Suez, provided an incentive for the Soviets to "fish in the troubled waters" of the Arab World. Added instability to the region was created by the great bitterness between Arab and Jew from the Palestine War and the unconsummated peace.

New Arab voices of nationalism, if weak, were beginning to be heard. In April, 1950, the Syrian Minister of National Economy advocated a non-aggression pact with the Soviet Union. Members of the Syrian Parliament called for closer ties with the Soviet Union as a counter-weight to what they felt was an anti-Arab policy on the part of the United States and Britain. The Egyptian Foreign Minister was also on record as favoring similar pro-Soviet moves.

The Tripartite Declaration

To cope with this destabilizing situation, Britain, France, and the United States agreed to coordinate their Middle East policy in the form of the Tripartite Declaration of May 25, 1950. In this document, the three major Western powers decided to act together to maintain the status quo in the region and to control the attempt by the Soviet Union to capitalize on the unrest there. The action by the three Western powers excluded the Soviet Union from diplomatic involvement in the oil-rich Middle East. More specifically, the Tripartite Declaration sought to maintain stability by controlling the flow of arms into the area and to avoid renewed hostilities by guaranteeing the armistice line—a move to reduce the temptation by local leaders to militarily change the de facto boundaries. Israel had no strong objections to the Western moves. The Arabs, however, reacted in anger to the Tripartite policy. Egypt, for instance, rejected the three-nation policy agreement and publicly criticized it as a Western attempt to perpetuate the British military bases in its country.

Israel, although having played no part in the creation of the Western policy, was happy with the boundary guarantees and the new Western policy implications of allowing Israel to receive arms equal to those shipped to the Arab states. The declaration, however, posed problems for Israel in terms of the already deteriorating friendship with the Soviet Union. The declaration, *inter alia*, affirmed U.S., British, and French expectations that the balanced military aid to both sides would make it possible for the Middle East "countries 'to play the role that falls on them in *the defense of the region as a whole*'"[14] (author's emphasis). The implication was that Israel would now play a role in defending the Middle East from a potential Soviet attack. The Israeli government correctly felt such a position would antagonize the Russians.

On the other hand, the guaranteed borders and the implication that it could now receive desperately needed arms from the West was most welcome. Commented an Israeli government spokesman:

> The Israeli Government presumes that the joint declaration by Britain, France, and the United States signifies the end of the discrimination which has hitherto been practiced in the supply of arms and military equipment to the Middle Eastern states. The Israeli Government notes with special satisfaction that the Governments of Britain, France, and the United States in loyalty to the United Nations, have declared their strong opposition to the use of force or the threat of force in the Middle East. This approach fully reflects the Israeli Government's policy.[15]

The Israelis felt compelled to record their approval of the Tripartate Declaration because it outlined a Western policy of great benefit to Israel's future survival in the face of anticipated Arab revenge.

The Soviet response was predictable in spite of Israel's efforts to play down the anti-Soviet implication of the declaration. The Soviet press now moved into high gear to criticize Israel's policy with increasing vengeance. Now Israel was not only characterized as leaning toward the West; it was referred to as a Western base of operations in the Middle East.

Yet the Soviets were not ready at this time to push for a major revision of big-power influence in the area. "It is significant that the Ministry of Foreign Affairs made no public statement on this declaration, a document which could be interpreted as assuming that the area was an exclusive field of operations of the West, and that the West, as the only supplier of armaments, had it in its power to regulate the supply of armaments to Israel and the Arab countries."[16]

The declaration, nevertheless, did have its impact on the individual national interests of states affected. It was conducive to a new alignment of states. The USSR found itself in a growing commonality of interests with Egypt—and in opposition to Israel—although at this time very little overt diplomatic action to develop this affinity was taken. As we will point out later, the Soviet commonality with Egypt, for instance, only increased as Moscow publicly supported Egypt's rejection of the 1951 Western invitation for membership in the proposed Allied Middle East Command—a regional defense organization aimed at keeping the Soviet Union out of the area.

Impact of Korean War on Middle East

One month after Britain, France, and the United States proclaimed the Tripartite Declaration, the Korean War broke out—the Communist government of North Korea launched a carefully prepared large scale military invasion of South Korea—with full clandestine support by the Soviet Union. The Western powers were alarmed. They had stopped threatened Soviet expansion in Western Europe. It now appeared that the Soviets were not only willing to push expansionist thrusts in non-European areas, they were even willing to assume all the risks involved in the use of conventional military forces to do so. Conceivably this was only a diversionary thrust with the major attack planned for the Middle East or Europe.

The international political impact of the Korean War had an adverse effect on Soviet–Israeli relations. In the first place, Israel was forced to confront the issue in the United Nations. The Security Council, in its second resolution (June 27), condemned the North Korean invasion as a breach of the peace under Chapter VII of the Charter. This called for UN collective security measures which were spelled out in the form of requests of member states to contribute military and other assistance to the Republic of Korea (South Korea) "as may be necessary to repel the armed attack and to restore international peace in the area." Since the USSR had walked out of the Security Council five months earlier in protest of the continued representation of Nationalist China instead of Communist China, the measure passed without a veto. Egypt, as a non-permanent member of the Security Council at this time, did not vote—presumably because of lack of instruction from Cairo—but later asked that its vote on this "crucial issue should be considered as an abstention."[17] The Egyptian action was very well received in Moscow.

Israel and the Korean War

For Israel, the United Nations encounter with the Korean invasion entailed some difficult choices. Israel had been admitted to the United Nations on May 11, 1949. For a time hereafter, Israel's UN policy was a low keyed "nonidentification" in the UN's "cold war" confrontations. This policy made Israel's participation in the United Nations reasonably acceptable to the Soviet Union. Yet a state identified so closely with religion—a religion basically embodying Western values—was restive under these restraints. Thus, beginning in the spring of 1950, Israel adopted a more active independent UN stance. Israel had recognized the People's Republic of China before the Korean War broke out. This was *a plus* in Moscow's view. The Korean War created some problems, however.

Foreign Minister Moshe Sharett characterized Israel's position on the Korean issue as an attempt to be neutral between East and West, but not to be neutral between peace and aggression. Said Sharett:

> The Israeli Government did not take sides in the grave conflict between Eastern Europe and the Western world. On the contrary, the principle of nonidentification with either of the blocs in the world to which Israel had adhered since the establishment of the State was being maintained. However, this principle of nonidentification should not be used for ignoring the case of peace, asserting the right of evading responsibility towards the United Nations, and become a weapon which instead of defending peace would affect the security of Israel itself.[18]

In line with the Security Council resolution of June 27, 1950, Secretary-General Trygve Lie, on June 29, contacted all members states asking for responses as to what contributions each would be prepared to make in support of the resolution. Israel at first only acknowledged receipt of the inquiry. However, later the inquiry did give rise to a special cabinet meeting, the results of which were communicated to the UN Secretariat on July 3. The Israeli cabinet's response to the UN was as follows:

> The Government of Israel opposes and condemns aggression wherever it may occur and from whatever quarter it may emanate . . . Israel supports the Security Council in its efforts to put an end to the breach of peace in Korea and to restore peace in the area.[19]

The cabinet position touched off considerable pressure in Israel. Action now shifted to the Knesset. Mapam and Communist members of the Israeli parliament submitted a no-confidence motion. The action was defeated 79 to 19, and Moshe Sharett then summarized the Israeli action as follows:

> The Israeli Government had borne in mind that the Security Council meeting was held without the U.S.S.R. However, al-

though the Israeli representatives had wholeheartedly encouraged efforts made by the U.N. General Secretariat to restore U.N. completeness (in representation), the Israeli Government could not agree to the view that the U.N.'s right to existence and its authority to act would cease with the exit of one of its members.[20]

Still, the Israeli government position in regard to the United Nations action in Korea was controversial for reasons of ideology, international law, and, especially, a liability to friendly relations with the Soviet Union. Obviously, the UN policy was bitterly resented by the Soviet Union, and Israel's policy would reap the Soviet wrath.

The Israeli press reflected the domestic division. *Haaretz* maintained that the United Nations should not submit to the North Korean aggression. It stated: "In proclaiming Israel's support of efforts to stop aggressive acts in Korea, our Government confirms the right of all people to freedom and of all countries to national independence."[21]

On the other hand, *Al-Hamishmar* maintained Israel should not support the Western bias reflected in the UN decision. The UN Security Council's action should be considered incomplete and illegal. Said *Al-Hamishmar*, "the Israeli Government must give a completely negative reply to the call for material and moral assistance to the Government of South Korea."[22]

As to be expected, the Israeli Communist newspaper, *Kol Ham*, stated that "the Israeli Government decision fully contradicts the Government's declared policy of nonidentification with any bloc."[23]

Later Walter Eytan, the Director-General of the Israeli Foreign Office, was to explain Israeli foreign policy as follows:

As Israel began to play an increasingly active part in the affairs of the United Nations, and as her representatives, showing neither fear nor favor, never hesitated to speak up on the burning problems of the hour, it became clear that Israel's foreign policy was set on a positive course, and that no merely negative term could adequately describe it. From that time, which may be put somewhere around the early summer of 1950, it seemed right to speak of Israel as pursuing an independent foreign policy, in other words, as having ideals of her own which she is prepared to advocate on their merits and defend against criticism, from whatever quarter it may come.[24]

Soviet Union Critical of Israel's Korean Policy

Eytan's statement was obviously directed against Soviet criticism of Ben Gurion's government on the Korean issue.

The Soviet press became exceedingly critical of Israel's position on Korea. *New Times* reported that:

> . . . Communist and Mapam deputies scathingly criticized the action of the cabinet and the leaders of the Mapai, the reactionary ruling party. Their support of the American aggressors was rightly characterized as an "anti-national act" and as a surrender to the ringleaders of the North-Atlantic bloc.[25]

Meanwhile Moscow Radio hailed the Egyptian stand on Korea. "Cairo political circles as well as the Egyptian press," said the media, "welcome the Egyptian Government's refusal to give support to American aggression in Korea."[26] As indicated before, Egypt's refusal to contribute to the UN effort in Korea was in protest to the continued British military presence in Egypt.

For Israel, the UN Korean episode had further adversely affected relations with the USSR. As if to compensate for its pro-American position, Israel now voted with the Soviet Union against the American position on the admission of the People's Republic of China to the UN. Israel again voted with the Soviet Union against the United States on the question of relations with Spain. But this did not soothe Soviet feelings.

Korea was seen as more important than whatever Israel might do in reference to voting on China and Spain.

Outside of the United Nations, the outbreak of the Korean War further added to Israel's dilemma of deteriorating relations with Russia. The governments of the major Western powers considered the invasion of Korea as an indication that the Communists were now willing to resort to military means to achieve their ends. Washington considered the building of a containment alliance in the Middle East as most urgent. The task, however, was complicated by the Arab-Israeli antagonism and the nationalists' restiveness under what they considered colonial domination by the West. British troops were still in Egypt and the Sudan. Israel was seen as a Western creation to break up the Arab unity movement, which was symbolized by the Arab League created in early 1945.

Post-War Anglo-Egyptian Relations

The conflict between Western objectives in the Middle East and the Arab states' interests (as seen by the nationalists) is well illustrated by the record of post-war Anglo-Egyptian relations up to this time. Almost immediately after World War II, Egypt requested a revision of the 1936 Anglo-Egyptian treaty. Egypt had felt the sting of British strong-arm tactics in its internal politics—tactics which the British defended on the basis of the treaty commitments.

The Saadist Party leader, Sidki, upon becoming prime minister in February, 1946, had made a carefully planned attempt to negotiate a treaty revision with the British. Sidki put together a negotiating team representing all the major political groups except the Wafd party.[27]

Sidki returned from London with the signed Sidki–Bevin Treaty embodying compromises and some deliberately vague provisions necessary to cover up the differences which could not be reconciled. In the treaty Britain had agreed to withdraw all its troops from the various locations in Egypt and limit them to the Canal Zone by the end of March, 1947. Furthermore, by September, 1949, the military forces would leave the Suez Canal Zone too. Egypt, for its part, would continue the Anglo-Egyptian alliance. With regard to the Sudan, the vague phraseology of the treaty appeared to be contradictory. On the one hand it referred to "unity of the Nile under the Egyptian crown," while on the other hand recognizing the right of the Sudan to "national self-determination."

In the end, because of the opposition of the Wafd party and the Muslim Brotherhood, Sidki was unable to ratify the treaty and he resigned. His successor, Premier Nokrashi, decided on an alternative approach. He appealed, in July, 1947, to the United Nations Security Council for the removal of British troops, charging that their presence in Egypt endangered the maintenance of international peace and security.

Finally, the United Nations failed to support the Egyptian contention. This second failure only added to Egypt's bitterness against the West—a bitterness which became an opportunity for the Soviets to seize the initiative in gaining inroads into the Middle East. That it would require the abandonment of Israel was no great liability, since calculations of national interests, not principles or ideology, was the basic motivation for Soviet policy decisions in the radical switch in Soviet policy from pro-Israel to pro-Arab. In a sense, the Soviet Union's gradual abandonment of Israel at this time represented a configuration of (1) the Soviet consciousness of new political opportunities in drawing closer to Arab nationalist leaders (which could significantly be done only if the commonality against Israel, the enemy, were also shared with the Arabs), (2) the rising frustration of Arab national leaders with Western colonialism as they saw it, (3) the continued Arab–Israeli conflict, and (4) the prevailing "cold war" between East and West in which the latter perceived the Korean attack as an indication of the Soviet Union's new predisposition to use military means for expansionist attempts.

Egyptian Nationalism

Egypt played a crucial role in the events which were to cause the Soviets to abandon Israel, and it is worthwhile to elaborate its internal politics at this time. The Sidki–Bevin agreement of 1946 had proved futile; the United Nations efforts of 1947 were a failure; the Arab-Israeli War of 1948–49 ended in humiliation and defeat for Egypt. Saadist Premier Nokrashi was assassinated in December, 1948, allegedly by members of the Muslim Brotherhood; the Supreme Guide of the Muslim Brotherhood, Hassan al Banna, was in turn assassinated in February, 1949—an assassination allegedly plotted by Prime Minister Abdel Hadi who succeeded Nokrashi when the latter was felled by the assassin's bullet. King Farouk's popularity was at a low ebb. The year, 1950, began under very trying circumstances for the government in Cairo. "Egypt consisted of a hated King, a hated Government, and a sullen, docile people permeated by groups plotting rebellion in secret. The end was near. It only required the folly of the King and a new period of Wafd misrule to bring it about."[28]

Farouk had previously found the Wafd party, although it was the biggest party in Egypt, so obstinate that he called upon rival political leaders to form a government. Now, in January of 1950, however, the Wafd came to the conclusion that its opposition role was no longer as appealing and decided to be more amenable to working with the king. Farouk, from the perspective of his own deteriorating situation, could no longer afford the luxury of opposing the Wafd's leadership of government in the situation of rising political violence. King Farouk called for elections, the Wafd party again won a majority of seats in the Chamber of Deputies, and Nahas Pasha, the Wafd leader, became premier. Public confidence fell to new lows as bribery and corruption became increasingly more evident. Late in 1950 Premier Nahas announced his determination to pressure the British troops out of Egypt and to refuse any compromise on the unity of the Nile under

'WHICH WAY DID YOU TWIST IT?'

Crockett in The Washington Star

The success of Iran's Mohammed Mossadeq in "twisting the British lion's tail" by nationalizing the British owned Anglo–Iranian Oil Company had considerable appeal to the Wafd government (and later to the Nasser regime) in Egypt in its on-going conflict with the continued British military presence there. (Crockett in The Washington Star)

Egyptian ultimate authority.

This proved to be on collision course with the rising American and British determination, after the outbreak of the Korean War, to increase Western military capability in the Middle East. The British, with United States support, were now even more reluctant to acquiesce to rising Egyptian demands for the removal of British military forces from Suez. Britain had treaty rights (the Anglo-Egyptian Treaty of 1936) to remain in Egypt until 1956. The problem was that the British felt it imperative to extend that deadline, and the Egyptians insisted 1956 was too long.

The situation generated a great deal of diplomatic activity. At one point Egypt proposed the solution that it be allowed to join NATO.[29] The United States opposed this request because "it would be undesirable to extend the Treaty any further. . . . The Treaty itself is limited to European States."[30] In the fall of 1950 Britain and the United States continued extensive discussions to formulate a common policy toward Egypt concerning the Suez base. One alternative the two Western powers considered was transferring the huge British military facility from Suez to the Gaza Strip. To be a reliable base, it would require Israel's voluntary consent which, reasoned the British and American decisionmakers, might be forthcoming if it were coupled with an Egyptian-Israeli peace treaty—an important objective among Israel's priorities. As an enticement to Egypt, the offer could be coupled with the evacuation of the Suez base. This proposal, although very optimistic in retrospect, would be doubly rewarding. It would be a solution to the threatened Soviet expansion in the Middle East as well as eliminating the Arab–Israeli impass which was creating so much difficulty for Western efforts to deal with the cold war threat in the Middle East.[31] In the end, the "Gaza plan" was dropped because the rapidly moving events of the Middle East relegated it to obsolescence before it could be seriously pushed.

The Proposed Middle East Defense Organization

In 1951 President Truman's administration decided to press for a Middle East defense organization. Hopefully this would be done in a manner acceptable to Egypt by converting the British troops in the Suez Canal Zone into a multilateral force, with Egyptian military participation as a fully equal partner. Through United States initiative the plan evolved into what was called the Allied Middle East Command, supported by the additional governments of Great Britain, France, Turkey, and Egypt, with the latter being the first Arab state to be invited as a founding member. It was assumed that the other Arab states would join later. The proposal for the Allied Middle East Command noted that Egypt's future lay with the free world and, consequently, it had an important role to play in the defense of "democratic nations" under the threat of Communist expansion. According to the proposal, Egypt's participation would be rewarded by British willingness to revise the Anglo-Egyptian Treaty of 1936 in terms of the withdrawal of all its forces from Egypt except those incorporated in the Allied Middle East Command.

As elaborated, the Allied Middle East Command would also be beneficial to Middle East states in terms of economic aid for social and economic advancement. The organization's primary purpose was to defend the Middle East against external aggression; it was not to deal with intra-Middle East quarrels such as the Arab–Israeli conflict.

The perspective of Egypt was considerably different. It did not share the Western concerns embodied in the regional defense proposal. Most of the Arab states, led by Egypt, had not supported the United Nations' Korean policy which was strongly influenced by the United States. Rather, the Arabs were very much a part of the creation of an informal neutral bloc which appeared in the United Nations in December, 1950. The United Nations' role in the creation of Israel, and the unsatisfactory experience Egypt had received at the hands of the Security Council in the 1947 protest were not unrelated to the stand the Arabs had now decided to take. The Soviets and the Arabs became conscious of a common alignment in the direction of their foreign policies. By the end of 1950, Soviet broadcasts to the Arab World in Arabic increased.[32] The targets were the Arab national liberation movements in their struggle against Anglo-American imperialism.

In October, 1951, the four states of the United States, Great Britain, France, and Turkey extended an invitation to Egypt to join the proposed Allied Middle East Command. Nahas Pasha's Wafd-led government of Egypt turned down the invitation. Not only did it reject Egypt's membership in the Middle East defense organization, it used the occasion to unilater-

'Now Listen—!'

Iran had already given "eviction notice" to the British (spring, 1951) in the form of voting to nationalize the British oil company in Iran. The Wafd government of Egypt decided to unilaterally abrogate the Anglo–Egyptian Treaty of 1936 on October 8 of the same year—an act which the British found unacceptable. The "silent Sphinx" refused to respond to British protests. (Reprinted with permission from The Buffalo Evening News)

ally abrogate (1) the 1899 Anglo-Egyptian Treaty establishing the joint control over the Sudan and (2) the Anglo-Egyptian Treaty of 1936.

The issues were now clearly drawn. The Western democracies were intent upon organizing a regional defense alliance in the Middle East to cope with the danger of Soviet expansion in that area. The Arab states generally, and Egypt in particular, had weighted its decision in favor of opposition to the proposal, which was considered as an *increase* in Western colonialism rather than as an organization needed to check Soviet expansionist threats. The Soviet Union was most appreciative of Egypt's decision and, consequently, began to take an active interest in supporting Egypt against the British military presence. The Soviet Union strongly opposed the creation of a Middle East regional military pact under Western auspices.

Israel was now caught in events hardly of its own making. It could not satisfy the Arabs' demands, for its very existence was at stake. On the other hand, the Western efforts in creating a Middle East alliance were opposed by both the Soviet Union and the Arab national leadership, as represented by, for instance, the Wafd party in power in Egypt. The USSR and the Arab leaders now each possessed the opportunity to satisfy the other's concern and to gain through cooperation for common interests. The Arabs could refuse to join the West's urgent efforts toward a defense alliance against the Soviets; the Soviet Union could abandon Israel, so strongly hated by the Arabs, and give the Arabs diplomatic support and material aid against their regional enemy. The Arabs, not Israel, seemed to be holding the trump cards.

NOTES

1. A.R.C. Bolton, *Soviet Middle East Studies: An Analysis and Bibliography* (Royal Institute of International Affairs and Oxford University Press, June, 1959), pp. 4–5.

2. Avigdor Dagan, *Moscow and Jerusalem* (New York: Abelard–Schuman, 1970), p. 40.

3. Ibid., p. 41.

4. Ibid.

5. Mordeckkai Namir later became the Secretary General of the Histadrut (Israel Trade Unions Organization).

6. Dagan, p. 42.

7. Ibid.

8. United Nations General Assembly, Plenary Meeting of the General Assembly, *Official Records*, May 11, 1949. The speaker was Polish Representative Drohojewski.

9. Yaacov Ro'i, "The Soviet Union, Israel and the Arab-Israel Conflict," *The U.S.S.R. and the Middle East,* eds. Michael Confino and Shimon Shamir (Jerusalem: Israel University Press, 1973), p. 136.

10. Ibid.

11. *New York Times*, November, 19, 1949, p. 2.

12. Dagan, p. 45.

13. *New York Times*, April 16, 1949, p. 2

14. *Jerusalem Post,* May 26, 1950, p. 1.

15. Foreign Radio Broadcasts, *Daily Report*, No. 103, May 26, 1950, p. 1.

16. Isaac London, "Evolution of the USSR's Policy in the Middle East," *Middle East Affairs,* 7 (May 1956): 173.

17. United Nations, *Everyman's United Nations* (7th ed.; New York: United Nations, 1964), p. 100.

18. Foreign Radio Broadcasts, *Daily Report*, No. 129, July 5, 1950, p. 1.

19. *Jerusalem Post,* July 3, 1950, p. 1.

20. Foreign Radio Broadcasts, *Daily Report*, No. 129, July 5, 1950, p. 1.

21. Ibid., No. 130, July 6, 1950, p. 1.

22. Ibid., No. 128, July 3, 1950, p. 2.

23. Ibid., No. 130, July 6, 1950, p. 3.

24. Walter Eytan, "Israel's Foreign Policy and International Relations," *Middle Eastern Affairs,* II (May, 1951), pp. 156–157.

25. Notes on "International Life," *New Times,* No. 28 (October, 1950), p. 20.

26. Foreign Radio Broadcasts, *Daily Report*, No. 129, July 5, 1950, p. 7.

27. The Wafd Party refused to prticipate because, since it was the largest in Egypt, it demanded a leading role in the negotiation team. Because the

Wafd was at irreconcilable odds with King Farouk at this time, the latter had asked Sidki of the Saadist Party to form a government.

28. Tom Little, *Modern Egypt* (New York: Frederick Praeger, 1947), p. 179.

29. "The Near East, South Asia and Africa," *Foreign Relations of the United States*, V, 1950, p. 306.

30. Ibid., p. 307.

31. Ibid., p. 298.

32.   Karmi Shweitzer, "Soviet Policy Towards Israel, 1946–1952," *Mizan*, XI (January–February, 1969), p. 25.

CHAPTER 8

Israel: Innocent Victim Between Western Containment Politics and Stalin Succession Politics

Even though the West had received a serious setback by Egypt's action in October of 1951, it decided to press on with the building of the defense alliance. Prime Minister Winston Churchill visited Washington in January, 1952. The two countries jointly reaffirmed their resolve that "an Allied Middle East Command should be set up as soon as possible" in order "to promote the stability, peaceful development, and prosperity of the countries of the Middle East."[1]

Impact of the New Eisenhower Administration

In the United States, the new Republican administration under Eisenhower took office in January, 1953. Within three months the new Secretary of State, John Foster Dulles, took a trip to the Middle East to size up the possibilities. His findings suggested a modification of the original proposals. To the Arabs generally, and to Egypt in particular, Dulles noted, the existence of Israel in Palestine was of greater concern than the fear of Communism and Soviet expansion. There was, however, a somewhat greater understanding of the Soviet threat in those countries located along the "northern tier" of the Middle East. Also, the issues of colonialism and British troops in Egypt were so important to Egypt that it was very unlikely Nasser would take his country into any Western controlled defense organization.

John Foster Dulles

Secretary of State John Foster Dulles (right) conferring with President Dwight D. Eisenhower at the Summer White House, in Denver, Colorado, September 7, 1953. (Courtesy, Wide World Photos)

John Foster Dulles was born in Washington, D.C., Feb. 25, 1888. The family roots extended back along a distinguished line of public servants and church leaders. John, his critics charged, all too often was confused as to which role was his.

He served as the fifty-third Secretary of State from January, 1953, to April, 1959, in the Eisenhower administration. Earlier, Governor Thomas Dewey had appointed him Senator from New York to fill the unexpired term of Senator Robert Wagner (July, 1949, to January, 1951).

His maternal grandfather, General John Watson Foster, was Secretary of State in President Benjamin Harrison's administration. Secretary of State Robert Lansing, in Wilson's administration, was his uncle (by marriage). Other ancestors included United States Minister to Great Britain John Welsh (1877–1879) and Joseph Dulles, a founder of the Academy of Sciences in Philadelphia. His father, Allen M. Dulles, was a Presbyterian minister in Watertown, New York, and later joined the faculty of Auburn Theological Seminary.

John Foster Dulles graduated valedictorian from Princeton University in 1908. Law, international affairs, and (later) religion served to attract his interest. As a secretary in the American delegation to the Second Hague Peace Conference (1907), he experienced his first major international conference. Other diplomatic experiences included a pre-World War I diplomatic assignment to Panama concerning cooperation in defense of the canal; assignment to the U.S. delegation at the Versailles Peace Conference; the American representative on the Reparations Commission; assignment to Poland (1927) as an advisor in administering the Polish Plan of Monetary Stabilization; posts as member of Senator Vandenberg's staff at the San Francisco founding conference of the United Nations (spring, 1945); member of the U.S. delegation to the United Nations General Assembly in 1946, 1947, 1948, and 1950; member of Secretary of State George Marshall's staff to the Moscow Council of Foreign Ministers meeting (March, 1947); and the negotiation of the peace treaty with Japan in 1951. The culmination of his career in international affairs occurred when President Eisenhower selected him to be Secretary of State.

During his tenure as Secretary of State, an armistice was achieved in Korea, but the proposed objective of "rolling back the iron curtain" in central Europe was a failure—a failure with embarrassment because Dulles' implied American aid to Soviet satellite states attempting to throw off the Russian yoke had to be faced in the East German anti-Communist riots of 1953, the Polish workers uprising (June, 1956), and, especially, the Hungarian revolt in fall, 1956, which was crushed by Soviet troops. The Geneva Conference on Indo-China (1954) was inconclusive at best. Dulles also emphasized defensive military pacts for the containment of the Soviet Union. Yet the Baghdad Pact in the Middle East polarized the area—especially antagonizing Egypt.

Nevertheless, the Middle East events of 1956 must have been the most disappointing to Secretary of State Dulles. His moralizing of the East-West conflict was a "made-to-order" situation for Nasser to play the "positive neutralist" position to maximize leverage against the West. Dulles became particularly annoyed when he felt Egypt was brazenly playing this strategy with the U.S. offer to finance the Aswan High Dam. As a result, the U.S. offer was suddenly and dramatically withdrawn on July 19, 1956, to make the point. In response Nasser nationalized the Suez Canal, which was seen as an intolerable threat to the vital interests of America's NATO allies, Britain and France. The event set in motion a chain of foreign policy disasters for the Western alliance. These events—when he led United States policy to side with the Soviets against America's NATO allies—became the nadir of Dulles' long and distinguished career in international affairs.

"Seeing the world through moralizing lenses" proved to be a dangerous habit which the man had developed over the years. His father was a Presbyterian minister. His approach to international relations had always had a moralizing strain going back all the way to experiences as a nineteen-year-old Princeton senior at the Second Hague Peace Conference. The basic legalistic-moralistic approach to politics was essentially the cadence of the social gospel—the optimistic idea of human progress found in the mainstream of American Protestantism at the time.

John Foster Dulles was elected chairman of the

Commission on a Just and Durable Peace—a creation, in 1941, of the Federal Council of Churches and supported by seven additional interdenominational church agencies. Out of power, his moralistic pronouncements caused few problems. However, after becoming Secretary of State, the moralizing created considerable liabilities as compromises and trade-offs became necessary. It was never very clear whether the moral pronouncements of the Secretary of State were only conscious public relations gimmicks or whether Mr. Dulles genuinely accepted his role as God's chosen among the sinners in international life.

In private life he became the senior partner in the prestigious New York law firm of Sullivan and Cromwell (with specialization in international law).

Personal tragedy finally came in the middle of Eisenhower's second term when the Secretary of State was confronted with terminal cancer. John Foster Dulles died on May 24, 1959.

Dulles, therefore, in June, 1953, decided to bypass Egyptian opposition and push for the "northern tier" pact. This decision only further aggravated Nasser and moved Moscow and Cairo toward a greater commonality of policy. Nasser aspired to the leadership role of the Arab states. Dulles' new diplomatic effort emphasizing Iraq was bitterly resented by Nassar as a "divide and rule" thrust which nullified his role in Egypt as head of the Arab nationalist movement.

Turkey, being allowed to join NATO, now agreed to participate in bringing the defense organization into being. On February 24, 1955, the Baghdad Pact was born in the Treaty of Mutual Cooperation between Iraq and Turkey. Britain, Pakistan, and Iran joined (in that order) later in 1955. The United States never officially joined, yet it gave the pact behind-the-scenes leadership. Other Arab states were expected to join since membership was specifically open to "any member of

"How's that for tossing a bouquet, huh?"

On the one hand the Eisenhower administration sought to win over the uncommitted nations with good will; on the other hand, Secretary of State John Foster Dulles felt threats were also in order to punish third world states that antagonized the West. Haynie in The Greensboro (N. C.) Daily News, *portrays the contradictory policy toward non-aligned states of the third world.*

the Arab League or any other state actively concerned with security and peace" in the Middle East.

However, "thunder from the streets," especially inspired by Egypt's antagonism to the pact, kept the other Arab states from membership. Dulles was well aware of the necessity of forbidding Israel to join if Arab states were to be included in the defense organization. Consequently, Israel was successfully barred by the innocent phrase in the original Turco–Iraqi treaty which allowed for the other states to join providing they were "fully recognized" by both Turkey and Iraq.

Israel Requests Reparations from East Germany

But what was happening diplomatically between Israel and the Soviet Union during the Western push for a Middle East defense organization? On January 16, 1951, Israel presented to the Soviet Union a note regarding the German reparations to Israel. The note was handed to M. L. Moukhine, the Soviet Chargé d'Affaires in Tel Aviv.[2] It set forth the Israeli position that Israel was entitled to German reparations from the Soviet occupied sector. Other similar notes were sent to the United States, Britain, and France. The Soviet Union ignored the note despite Israeli reminders sent in October and November in 1951.

On January 29, 1951, the Soviet Union rejected the nomination of Zalman Shazar as Israeli Minister to Moscow because of his Zionist background in Tsarist Russia and his popularity with the Jewish intelligentsia in the Soviet Union.[3]

On January 30, 1951, the Knesset voted approval of the Israeli Government's negotiations with the United States for "Point Four" aid. The vote was 56 to 29 with six abstentions.[4] The Knesset also defeated by large majorities a left-wing proposition that, in effect, called for a policy of closer alignment with the Soviet Union.[5] Moshe Sharett attacked Mapam and Communist Knesset members who had criticized the government for its inclinations toward the West.[6]

In April and May, 1951, the Soviet delegate at the UN abstained from discussions in the Security Council regarding mutual Syrian and Israeli complaints. Tsarapkin, the Soviet delegate to the UN, also abstained from voting on the Suez resolution in September, 1951.

Soviets Critical of Israel

In July, 1951, the Soviet press accused Israel of being a base of American imperialism. Israeli rulers were labeled as nationalistic and bourgeois.[7] The Soviet press published a report on a new military pact between Israel and Turkey. Moshe Sharett felt compelled to ask the head of the Soviet diplomatic mission in Israel to deny the report. However, the Soviets were saying something different at the diplomatic level. In the same month Gromyko assured Minister Eliashiv, who was sent to Moscow instead of Shazar, that there was "no reason why relations between the Soviet Union and Israel should not be normal."[8]

The Soviet press was also attacking Turkey because she was considering the possibility of joining NATO. Both Turkey and Israel were considered as bases of American imperialism. The United States–British-proposed Allied Middle East Command substantiated Soviet doubts about Israel and Turkey. After Turkey joined NATO, Israel was informed by the Western powers of their decision to create the Middle East defense alliance. Israel was also informed that Egypt was invited to participate as a founding member. The Israeli press reported on October 18, 1951, that Israel had not been invited to join the Middle East defense organization.[9] Israel, the press speculated, found itself in a dilemma; if Egypt decided to join as a founder-member and Israel refused to join, Egyptian military power would be enhanced at Israeli expense. And if Israel joined the proposed pact, it would invite an open conflict with the Soviet Union. Israel must have realized that the proposed pact would not materialize because Egypt was anti-British. It was also clear to Jerusalem that Egypt would not join any pact in which Israel would be an ally.

On November 21, 1951, Acting Soviet Foreign Minister, Andrei Gromyko, handed the envoys of the Middle East countries, including Israel, a note on the proposed anti-Soviet alliance.[10] The note denounced the establishment of the Allied Middle East Command as an act of aggression against the Soviet Union. Israel sent its reply in a note on December 8, 1951, which was read by Prime Minister Ben Gurion to the Knesset on February 27, 1952. The note stated:

> . . . Israel has never agreed and will not agree to support aggressive activities or plans aimed against the USSR or any other peace-loving country . . . .
>
> . . . The return of Jewish exiles to their Homeland was the destiny of Israel and implied that the ban on Jewish emigration from Russia was inconsistent with the Soviet policy of equality and the right of self-determination for all nations.[11]

On December 23, 1951, Foreign Minister Moshe Sharett met the Soviet Foreign Minister Vyshinsky at the meeting of the foreign ministers in Paris. Although the agenda was not revealed, it was reported that the proposed Allied Middle East Command and the immigration of Soviet Jewry to Israel were discussed.[12]

The Slansky Trial

Israel's relations with Eastern Europe also continued to deteriorate—especially with Czechoslovakia regarding the Slansky trial in November, 1952. Rudolf Slansky, a former Deputy Premier of Czechoslovakia who was of Jewish background, ex-Foreign Minister Vladimir Clementis, and thirteen others were accused of espionage and sabotage in Czechoslovakia. Moshe Sharett, the Israeli Foreign Minister, read a statement in the Knesset regarding the Slansky trial on November 24, 1952.

... The Government of Israel holds it utterly superfluous to attempt any detailed and factual denial of the issue of libels and fabrications regarding the activities of its members and emissaries, produced by the fertile imagination of the Czechoslovak Secret Police and Public Prosecution ... .[13]

Rude Pravo, the official organ of the Czechoslovak Communist Party, opened an editorial offensive against Zionism and Israel, condemning Israel in the context of the cold war rhetoric of the time:

The State of Israel has become a base of American imperialism against the Arab countries and the People's Democracies by placing spies and subversive agents in those countries. The diplomats of the bourgeois State of Israel have become spies on the payroll of American imperialists and have organized a diversion in the Czechoslovak Republic on behalf of their American employers, causing Czechoslovakia serious harm.[14]

Miloslav Patek, a commentator on Prague Radio, announced:

The trial showed that it is no coincidence that Zionism became the servant of the U.S. imperialism .... Its main center remains in the United States despite the setting up of the capitalist state of Israel. ... In order to camouflage this real role of the State of Israel, it was agreed at the same time that Israel would on a few occasions oppose the U.S. voting machine at the United Nations as a so-called neutral state. By this trick the Israeli politicians hoped to gain the confidence of peace-loving mankind.[15]

The Israeli–East European relations deteriorated further with the expulsion of Dr. Kubovy, the Israeli Minister in Poland and Czechoslovakia.[16] Zionist leaders were also arrested in Hungary.[17]

Stalin and the Jewish "Doctors Plot"

An even greater shock in Israeli diplomatic relations came with the announcement of the Jewish "doctors plot" in the Soviet Union in January, 1953. Five of the nine accused doctors were Jews. Moscow asserted that these doctors had murdered the Secretary of the Central Committee of the Communist Party, Andrei Zhdanov, and the Secretary of the Moscow Committee of the Party, General Alexander Shcherbakov[18] (who was also in charge of the political administration of the Soviet army during World War II). Moscow also claimed that the doctors tried to kill Marshall A. M. Vassilevsky, a member of the party's Central Committee; Marshall Ivan Koniev, former commander of the Soviet ground forces; General of the Army Shtemenko, one time Chief of the General Staff; and Admiral P. J. Levhenko, Deputy Minister of the Navy.[19]

It is interesting to note that this diplomatic shock wave had its roots in the importance Israeli foreign policy attached to the right of Jews to be allowed to immigrate to Israel, and in the sensitivity with which the Communist states of Eastern Europe—particularly the Soviet Union—viewed nationalistic divisiveness within its domestic affairs.

The Soviet press seized the opportunity to attack Israel. V. Minayev stated:

> . . . The leading figures in the Israeli government, Ben Gurion, Sharett, Shiloah [organizer of the Israeli intelligence] and other leaders, carry out the instructions of the State Department. Their close political ties with the American imperialists find expression in the support they render Washington's aggressive policy in the international arena. . . . The Zionist leaders, who govern the state of Israel, conduct a campaign of slander against the Soviet Union and its policy of promoting peace and friendship among nations.[20]

Moshe Sharett declared in the Knesset on January 19, 1953:

... The government of Israel has regarded friendship of the
U.S.S.R. as one of the assets of its international position and as a
source of gratification for the whole Jewish people. It views with
deep sorrow and grave anxiety the pernicious anti-Jewish course
officially adopted in the U.S.S.R., which must arouse vehement
indignation on the part of the State of Israel and the Jews
throughout the world. . . .[21]

On February 9, 1953, the Soviet Legation in Tel Aviv was
bombed. In view of the rising antagonism in Soviet–Israeli
relations, the Jerusalem government immediately condemned
"the dastardly outrage committed this evening at the Soviet
Legation in Tel Aviv." In apologizing to the Soviet Union, the
government expressed its "profound sense of affliction and
deep regret. . . .[22] The situation, triggered by the Slansky trial
and the "doctors plot," had deteriorated much faster and more
dangerously than could have been anticipated. What began as
a protest was now threatening overall Israeli national interests
in relation to the Soviets. In this context Prime Minister Ben
Gurion, on February 10, 1953, gave a full account of the event
to the Knesset. Ben Gurion denounced the incident before the
Israeli legislature and implied that it might create further
liabilities for Israel if the trend were not reversed.[23] Thus, Ben
Gurion declared the government's interest in maintaining
normal relations with, as he phrased it, "every peace-loving
country."[24] There was no doubt he was referring to the Soviet
Union.

On February 12, 1953, the break came. Using the legation
bombing as a pretext, Andrei Vyshinsky summoned the Israeli
Minister in Moscow, Shmuel Eliashiv, and informed him of
the breaking of diplomatic relations with Israel. P. Yershov,
the Soviet Minister in Israel, was ordered home. The Soviet
note of Vyshinsky to Eliashiv mentioned Moshe Sharett's
speech in the Knesset on January 19, 1953, in which it was
said that Prime Minister Sharett "openly invited hostile activities against the Soviet Union."[25]

The *Jerusalem Post* viewed the drastic Soviet action as

stemming from its sensitivity to rising Jewish nationalism in the Soviet Union's domestic affairs[26]—a situation helped along by Israel's determined foreign policy objective of encouraging Soviet Jews to immigrate to Israel.[27]

The status of Soviet Jews was, nevertheless, not solely responsible for Moscow breaking diplomatic relations. The new opportunities in developing rapport with the Arab leadership was an element in the anti-Israel action. It represented "tacking the Soviet ship of state" to see what opportunities might arise from siding with the Arab world in its hatred of Israel and charges of Western colonialism. Not the least of the charges of colonialism stemmed from the recent Western efforts at extending NATO's southern flank to contain the Soviet Union in the Middle East—a situation taking renewed urgency from the shock, to the West, of Communist military expansion in Korea.

This severance in diplomatic relations should not, however, be considered as a final switch of Soviet foreign policy from pro-Israel to pro-Arab. As a matter of fact, the official action to re-establish diplomatic relations with Israel was announced on July 20, 1953—only five months after the break. The secret initiative on the part of the Soviet government to restore relations shortly after Stalin's death came as a surprise to Israel. Foreign Minister Moshe Sharett found it so unexpected that he asked the Foreign Ministry to make a study to more convincingly explain the Soviet move. The study concluded that the friendly action by Moscow toward Israel was explained in the context of the Soviet "carrot" line—"the peace offensive"—after Stalin's death, of which the movement toward the Austrian peace treaty, the renunciation of territorial claims against Turkey and the normalization of relations with Yugoslavia were also a part.

The Nasser Coup in Egypt

In the early 1950s Moscow's reaction to events taking place on the Nile was of increasing concern to the West which, in

'THE FLIGHT FROM EGYPT'

The Nasser coup which toppled the King Farouk regime in Egypt (1952) was amazingly restrained in violence against the former rulers who had a reputation for corruption and bribery. The cartoon depicts a "bloated and loaded" Farouk sailing away "in style" from his native Egypt. (Wood in The Richmond News-Leader)

turn, was reacting to international affairs in the *Weltanschaaung* of the cold war. The Nasser coup in July, 1952, was *not* seen by the Soviet Union as an opportunity to move against the West. The reasons for this were many. Once in power, Nasser turned on the Egyptian Communists, in contrast to the loose cooperative understanding Nasser's clandestine organization had with the Cairo Communist group before the coup. Furthermore, right after the seizure of power, Nasser bent over backward in friendly gestures to the British (and Americans), for he felt the British military forces might be used to nullify the coup in a manner similar to the British military intervention in the Egyptian government in February, 1942. There may also have been apprehensions in Moscow lest the successful "rightist" military seizure of government delay rather than speed up the possible influence of the Soviet government in Egypt. In any case, the Nasser-Naguib coup created a vacillation between faint support and sharp criticism on the part of the Soviet press. The Nasser regime was characterized as reactionary, showing its true colors by the harsh persecution of the Egyptian people.[28] Soviet expert, L. N. Vatolina, as late as 1954, characterized the Nasser regime in Egypt as "madly reactionary, terrorist, anti-democratic, demagogic" in its policies.[29]

After the conclusion of the Anglo-Egyptian treaty of 1954, and when it appeared that Nasser had made his peace with the West, Moscow again publicly voiced criticism of Nasser, charging him with being a virtual puppet of Dulles and having sold out the national interest of Egypt and the Arab world. The Nasser government was also charged with violating the wishes of the masses. In a prophetic tone, the Soviet Academy of Science, in an article on Africa, concluded that "the Egyptian toilers would as yet have to fight many a struggle up to the victory of real democracy."[30]

In summary, after Nasser's acceptance of the new Anglo-Egyptian Treaty of 1954, Moscow became even more critical of Egypt's government than it had been of the Wafd government of 1950–1952. The pro-Nasser era of Soviet relations didn't come until 1955 after Cairo's basic foreign policy realignment.

However, the equivocal predicament of the Soviet Union

Gamal Abdul Nasser

President Gamal Abdul Nasser of Egypt at the African Heads of States meeting, Addis Ababa, Ethiopia, May 25, 1963. (Courtesy, The United Nations)

Nasser's family roots lay in the Nile farming village of Beni Moor near Assiut in Upper Egypt—a good 200 miles south of Cairo. Gamal Abdul Nasser was, however, born in Alexandria (January 15, 1918). His father, Abdul Nasser Hussein, having shown considerable promise as a boy, had been sent to the Coptic elementary school in Assiut from which he graduated with a primary school certificate. This made it possible for the father to get a job with the Egyptian postal service which, in turn, meant that he would be called upon to leave his home village to serve, by periodic transfers, wherever postal clerks were needed in Egypt.

In 1914 he was sent to the postal service in Alexandria where, in 1917, he married Fahima Hammad. It was here that Egypt's future President, Gamal, was born. The family moved to Assiut in 1921 and, two years later (1923), to the village of Khatabta on the edge of the Delta. Because the local school was felt to be inadequate, the seven-year-old Gamal was sent to an uncle to attend school in Cairo. While there, his mother, with whom he had been very close in his earlier childhood, died in 1926. This was an especially shocking experience to the young boy because the father decided not to inform Gamal, who found out about his mother's death only when he came home for a school vacation—after his father had remarried. Available evidence indicates this shock was a contributing factor to his rebellious nature as a youth. Already as a student in Alexandria, where he had been sent to continue his education, he participated in demonstrations. Once he was arrested and spent the night in an Alexandrian jail.

Gamal did not get along with his father. He was admitted to the military academy in Cairo in 1937, graduating a year later with the rank of Second Lieutenant. This set him off on a military career which proved to be of considerable satisfaction to the frustrated rebel of earlier years.

Gamal Abdul Nasser distinguished himself as a soldier in the Arab-Israeli war of 1948; he was wounded in one of the battles at the Faluja pocket. The war also made him aware of the extensive government corruption in his country. Egypt's humiliation, resulting from what he felt was considerable indifference to the war on the part of King Farouk and from the intimidating arrogance of the British military presence, only added to his indignation at the corruption in the highest levels of the Egyptian government.

This led to Nasser's initiative in creating a secret organization among junior grade officers, and it was this group which launched a successful coup against King Farouk's rule on July 23, 1952. For prestige purposes, the Free Officers (as the secret organization of junior grade officers called itself) used the popular Major-General Mohammed Neguib as a figure-head, which also promoted the image of legitimacy.

The Revolutionary Command Council, the new name which the Free Officers gave themselves after the coup, was somewhat unique in that it had seized power "without experience, program or ideology." Gamal Abdul Nasser and the other dozen members of the new ruling junta moved pragmatically to reduce corruption, promote social justice, modernize and develop Egypt, negotiate the British out of Egypt, and free the Arab world from what they considered to be Western colonialism. The challenge to the RCC included the ultimate unification of the Arab world under Egypt's leadership.

The creation of the Baghdad Pact and the continued American support for Israel put Egyptian-American relations on collision course, sending Nasser to Moscow for an alternative client relationship. The Soviet arms deal of 1955 and the Soviet backing in the 1956 war were payoffs, in his interpretation, of Egypt's national interests in the era of the East-West cold war.

By the time of his death, September 28, 1970, Nasser, disappointingly, had been only partially successful in realizing his goals. While the British military presence had been successfully negotiated out of Egypt, the elimination of corruption and the challenges of modernization and development in Egypt proved too protractive to be considered a success for the regime. Also, the challenges of Israel and Arab unity were far from satisfactorily resolved when the burdens of the office took their toll to the point where he suffered a fatal heart attack at age 52.

For the Egyptian nationalists and the many Arab nationalists throughout the Middle East, the handsome, charismatic Nasser had been a hero who would deliver them from their humiliation and poverty to a new era of self-respect and Arab greatness.

---

toward relations with Israel and the Arab world should be seen in the context of Nasser gradually establishing himself as the most aggressive leader of Arab nationalism and attempting to rid the Arab world of the last remnants of Western colonialism. Not only was Nasser at work getting the British military out and frustrating the Western efforts in the proposed Middle East defense alliance, he was also taking on the wrath of France by aiding Ben Bella's forces in Algeria.

The French struggle in Algeria flared into open civil war in 1954. Nasser was sympathetic and gave material aid to the Algerian nationalists. France reacted by agreeing to supply Egypt's arch enemy, Israel, with arms. In itself, this chain of events led Moscow to a more favorable view of Nasser.

Stalin's Death

As already mentioned, Stalin's death on March 5, 1953, was another important milestone in the Soviet switch toward a pro-Arab policy. Although Malenkov formally replaced Stalin as head of the Soviet government, Bulganin and Khrushchev very soon began eroding Malenkov's position and eventually replaced him in effective control of Soviet policy. Various important Middle East issues had to be faced. What should be done to counteract current Western efforts to create a Middle East organization directed against the Soviet Union? Secretary of State John Foster Dulles, as the representative of a new administration in Washington, met with G. Abdul Nasser in Cairo on May 11, 1953, to see if the Egyptian leader might be prevailed upon to ameliorate his previous opposition to a Middle East defense pact. An attempt was also made to approach Nasser about reconciliation in the Arab-Israeli dispute.

The new Soviet leadership was also confronted with the question of what to do about re-establishing relations with Israel—relations broken shortly before Stalin's death. Of increasing concern in Moscow was also the need to relate more carefully to the native nationalist, anti-colonial leadership in the third world.

On August 8, 1953, G. M. Malenkov, Chairman of the Council of Ministers of the USSR, reviewed Soviet foreign policy at the meeting of the Supreme Soviet of the USSR. He stated:

> . . . Desirous of lessening general tension, the Soviet Government consented to the re-establishment of diplomatic relations with Israel. In doing so, it was mindful of the fact that the Israeli Government had given an undertaking that "Israel would not be a party to any alliance or pact aiming at aggression against the Soviet Union." We believe that resumption of diplomatic relations will facilitate cooperation between the two states.[31]

However, Malenkov also made favorable references to the established Arab governments. "The assertion made by certain foreign newspapers," he said, "that resumption of diplomatic relations with Israel will tend to weaken the Soviet Union's relations with Arab states is devoid of foundation. The activities of the Soviet Government will be directed in the future, too, to furthering friendly cooperation with the Arab states."[32]

A hardening of the Soviet attitude against Israel's demands for the right of Jews to leave Russia was in evidence in late 1953. On November 29, 1953, Israeli Minister Eliashiv returned to his position in Moscow while the Soviet Minister, Aleksandr Abramov, arrived in Tel Aviv shortly thereafter. On

December 21, 1953, Eliashiv met with Soviet Deputy Foreign Minister Gromyko, and raised the question of immigration of Soviet Jews to Israel. This time the Russians were adamant. Gromyko explicitly told Eliashiv that the answer was *no* and the Soviet Union considered the issue closed.

Soviet Policy in the UN

The exigencies of Soviet Middle East policy at this time can also be traced in the United Nations. The Soviet Union's last important pro-Israel, anti-Arab action in the Security Council occurred in the Suez Canal issue of September 1, 1951, when the USSR did *not* veto the Western sponsored resolution requesting Egypt to allow Israeli ships to pass through the canal and the Strait of Tiran. Nevertheless, even at this time, the Soviet representative explained his vote as not being against either Israel or Egypt.

In the General Assembly session of 1952, the Soviet Union sought to organize its national objectives into meaningful policy positions on the plethora of UN agenda items concerning (1) the maintenance of international peace and security (January 12); (2) Southwest Africa (January 19); (3) the UN involvement in Korea (February 5); (4) the invitations to the People's Republic of China and the Democratic People's Republic of Korea to participate in the UN General Assembly discussions; (5) the UNRWA Director's report (November 6); (6) the Soviet sponsored resolution on freedom of information (December 16); (7) the Moroccan resolution (December 19); (8) the Trusteeship Council report (December 21); and (9) the resolution pertaining to underdeveloped countries (December 21). In each case, Israel cast a vote on the opposite side of the Soviet Union, yet in no instance did the USSR criticize the Israeli position. It is to be noted, however, that at least on some of these issues various Arab states also took a position on the opposite side.

On those UN issues which more or less directly affected Israeli interests in 1952, the Soviet Union usually abstained from voting, and it did not participate in the debate. For instance, on December 21, 1952, the General Assembly voted on an Israeli complaint concerning the Arab violation of the Armistice agreements through violent acts of infiltration; the Soviet bloc abstained. In October, 1953, the Security Council took up the Arab complaint of the bloody Israeli retaliatory raid against the Jordanian village of Qibya in which a number of Jordanian women and children were killed. The Soviet representative did not participate in the debate, did not vote, and refrained from even explaining his abstention.

As reflected in the United Nation's diplomacy, until 1954 there was little cause for Israeli concern about anti-Israeli policies on the part of the Soviet Union. The one exception—which evolved outside of UN politics—was the confrontation over the *aliyah* (the immigration of Jews to Palestine).

On January 22, 1954, the Soviet Union cast its first veto on a major Middle East question. The veto was on a French, British, and U.S. sponsored resolution which dealt with the Syrian–Israeli conflict over rights in the demilitarized zone. The Arabs (through the Lebanese member of the Security Council at that time) tended to oppose the Western resolution (S/3151/Rev. 2)[33] because they feared an erosion of Syrian rights via the large amount of authority the resolution gave to the Chairman of the Syrian–Israeli Mixed Armistice Commission.[34] In effect, the Soviet veto supported the Arab position—but only mildly so. Having cast the first Soviet veto on a Middle East resolution, the Soviet representative M. Vyshinsky, in explaining his vote, was somewhat on the defensive[35] after the British representative criticized the Soviet Union's action by saying: "All Mr. Vyshinsky wants to do, I think, is to muddy the waters, not to prevent any leaks."[36]

The Soviet Union's first clearly anti-Israel, pro-Arab action in the Security Council occurred two months later (March 29,

1954) when it vetoed a resolution (S/2298/Rev.1) which criticized Egypt for not having complied with the Security Council resolution of September 1, 1951 (S/2298/Rev.1), allowing Israeli shipping through the Suez Canal and the Strait of Tiran. The resolution again called upon Egypt to allow Israeli passage through the two waterways "in accordance with its obligations under the Charter. . . ."[37]

The veto required some public rationalization because the Soviet Union had *not* vetoed a similar resolution three years earlier. Vyshinsky explained his veto by saying (1) that the 1951 resolution had not achieved any positive results, and (2) that the Arab states opposed the resolution[38] (a position which the Arab states had also held in 1951). Even in the vetoing of the Western resolution against Egypt, Soviet representative Vyshinsky did not condemn Israel. Nevertheless, his explanation did coincide with the Egyptian and Lebanese arguments, and the speech was enthusiastically lauded by Egypt. March 29, 1954, was, therefore, another significant milestone in the movement of Soviet foreign policy from pro-Israel to pro-Arab.

The Israeli press did not take the Soviet veto very lightly. The *Jerusalem Post* commented:

> The veto itself could perhaps be understood, though not defended, against the background of naked power politics, the East-West conflict and the apparent Soviet wish to include the Middle East as a key area in the cold war and to increase tension there. . . .[39]

Haaretz claimed that the Soviet veto

> demonstrates the partiality of this strong power regarding the dispute between Israel and its neighbors . . . the new Soviet policy has direct influence on the stability of the region, and this influence is not in favour of stability.[40]

Al-Hamishmar went on to say that "with the application of the Soviet veto, Egypt has, from an international political viewpoint, scored an additional victory over Israel."[41]

By casting their veto in the UN Security Council, the Soviets most probably wanted a limited political victory for the Egyptians, since they were not sure about Egypt's position regarding the impending Middle East defense pact, the Baghdad Pact. As a matter of fact, the Soviets, on March 23, 1954, warned Egypt that it would consider the conclusion of any Western sponsored military pact "an unfriendly and even hostile act" against the Soviet Union. It was reported that Daniel Solod, the new Soviet ambassador to Egypt, had explained the Kremlin's attitude toward the Middle East defense pacts to Mahmoud Fawzi, the Egyptian Foreign Minister.[42]

If March 29, 1954, represented a major turning point in Soviet policy away from Israel, how can we explain what happened between September, 1951, when the USSR abstained in a similar UN resolution, and the March 29, 1954, Soviet (pro-Arab) act vetoing essentially the same Security Council resolution?

The change in policy over these three and a half years involved a certain amount of vacillation and "trial and error." The change reflected a cautious policy of opportunism in which the Arabs and the Israelis were re-measured as to whose support was most advantageous in realizing Soviet national interests in the world political arena. In the Arab states, the rise of native nationalist sentiment against the West was of obvious interest to Moscow. Egypt's refusal to accept membership in the Western proposed Allied Middle East Command in October, 1951, and its simultaneous unilateral abrogation of the old 1936 military defense treaty with Britain were not unnoticed in Moscow.

The Nasser coup in Egypt (July, 1952) was originally discounted by the Soviet Union because the coup leaders seemed to be somewhat pro-Western. However, when in August the Nasser-Neguib government declined to support the second Western attempt to build a Soviet containment alliance in the Middle East—the so-called Middle East Defense

Organization—it was looked upon with satisfaction by the Kremlin.

When Secretary of State John Foster Dulles (representing the new Republican administration which took office in January, 1953) made a renewed effort to seek a Middle East containment alliance in May, 1953, it met the same response in Cairo. With a more flexible situation in the Kremlin, now that Stalin had passed from the scene, a more serious consideration of Arab potential for Soviet interests occurred. It is now known that in October, 1953, the Soviet Union sent Ambassador Daniel Solod to Cairo with instructions to lay the groundwork for a possible pro-Arab Soviet Middle East foreign policy.

At the April 13, 1954, hearings before the U.S. House Committee on Foreign Affairs on the Mutual Security Act of 1954, Henry Byroade, Assistant Secretary of State for Near Eastern, South Asian, and African Affairs, asserted:

> Ever since I have had this job, I have wondered when Russia would take sides in the Arab-Israeli problem, and she has now clearly done that. She has vetoed twice, within the last 6 months, resolutions in the Security Council on this matter . . . I think their main policy is to veto, now, anything that appears to be constructive in the area toward relieving tensions.[43]

On May 3, 1954, Henry Byroade made a similar statement in which he reviewed Soviet foreign policy in the Middle East before the House Committee on Foreign Affairs. Byroade stated:

> There are now a number of indications that Soviet intentions are being focused to a new degree upon this part of the world. . . . I have been expecting this change of attitude to show itself within the United Nations. This has now happened. The Arab–Israeli conflict, so often before the United Nations, has until recently been free of abusive veto power of the Soviet Union. They have

now wielded their veto twice in succession on this matter in the Security Council.[44]

However, Byroade cautioned that:

> Many in the Arab world see this extension of the hand of Russia as a friendly move to take their side in the case against Israel. . . . I believe this facade of friendship to be indeed a motive of the Kremlin—but I believe it is only a byproduct of their real intentions. . . . The other, and this we see as their primary objective, is to stymie the United Nations in order to maintain and increase the dangerous tensions that exist within the area.[45]

Although, as we have indicated, the March 29, 1954, veto was a milestone in the Soviet policy switch away from Israel, it would be a mistake to represent it at this time as the proverbial "180 degree reversal." For example, when the Soviet Union in March, 1954, elevated its Cairo legation to the rank of embassy, the move was counterbalanced by a similar action in Israel.[46] Although the Soviet Union was adopting an anti-Israeli line at the UN, its bilateral diplomatic relations with Israel were not significantly affected. When in June, 1954, the USSR moved to raise its diplomatic relations with Israel to the ambassadorial level, many felt the act should be seen as a Soviet countermove to the development of friendly relations between Egypt and Britain at this specific time in the form of the impending agreement on the Anglo-Egyptian treaty of 1954. The Arab–Soviet relations had not, as yet, pre-empted Arab relations with the West inasmuch as the Arab states were still at this time hoping to get arms from the Western democracies to match the Israeli stockpiles of armaments.

The anti-Israel action in the UN by the Soviet Union was, however, a matter of deep apprehension to Israel. On May 10, 1954, Moshe Sharett, now the Israeli Prime Minister, made a major foreign policy statement to the Knesset in which the Soviet veto at the UN was denounced. Sharett stated:

> The line adopted by the Soviet Union in the Security Council to block by veto any proposal that is not acceptable to the Arabs

and to endorse their interests at every stage, raises serious problems. It threatens either to paralyze the Security Council as far as problems concerning the Middle East and Israel–Arab relations are concerned or to turn it into a one-sided instrument capable of action only against Israel . . . . This new attitude of the Soviet Government has helped to promote a trend in American policy, increasingly noticeable of late, towards supporting the Arab point of view and opposing that of Israel.[47]

Sharett mentioned the speeches of the U.S. Assistant Secretary of State, Henry Byroade, regarding the Middle East as an indication of American foreign policy toward Israel. "The Soviet veto," Sharett said, "acts today exactly in the same direction as does American readiness to grant arms to Iraq."[48] Israel was opposed to the United States' intention of supplying Iraq with arms if the latter joined the Turkish–Pakistani defense pact. Sharett also expressed Israel's desire to live in peace and, if possible, to maintain friendly relations with the Soviet Union despite deep-seated conflict over the relations of Soviet Jewry with Israel. Obviously Israel did not want the Arab states to enhance their relations with the Soviet Union at Israeli expense, even though serious disputes existed between the two countries.

The Anglo-Egyptian Treaty

On July 27, 1954, Egypt and Britain reached an initial agreement in which Britain would evacuate the Suez Canal Zone within twenty months.[49] The final agreement between Britain and Egypt regarding the Suez Canal was signed in October, 1954, with the United States acting as a mediator between the two countries. This American stand vis-a-vis Egypt was not welcomed by the Israelis.[50]

Israel and the Soviet Union both opposed the Suez Agreement, but for different reasons. Israel regarded the agreement as a severe blow to its own security, because Egypt might now turn to threatening or hostile activity against Israel in violation of the 1949 Rhodes Armistice Agreement. The British presence in the Canal was a buffer zone between Israel and Egypt. The Israeli press was also critical of the Anglo-Egyptian Suez agreement. *Haboker* indicated that the Suez Agreement placed Israel in a new situation. "Not only did the situation become more tense because of the superiority achieved by Egypt," claimed the paper, "but several things also cropped up meanwhile which added strength and impudence to the rulers of Cairo."[51] According to *Davar*, the crucial factor in these new developments was the United States, which promised "military aid to the Arab countries despite their open refusal to abandon their hostile intentions regarding Israel."[52]

On August 30, 1954, Israeli Prime Minister Moshe Sharett made a major foreign policy statement to the Knesset regarding the Anglo-Egyptian agreement. Emphasized Sharett:

> . . . There is no vestige of any concern whatever for the security of Israel in the . . . Agreement between Britain and Egypt. The document was framed as if Israel did not exist, as if no formal declaration at all had been made by Egypt asserting her determination to maintain a state of war against Israel, and as if no public threats to attack Israel had been uttered. . . .

Sharett warned that "Israel must guard against surprises which may call it to defend its security and forestall trouble."[54] The Knesset declared, "Israel will not reconcile herself to the policy of the U.S. and Britain with regard to the arming of the Arab states and ignoring Israel's security problems."[55] Sharett's foreign policy had the overwhelming support of the Knesset.

To upset the arrangement between Egypt on the one side, and the British and the Americans on the other side, an agency of the Israeli government organized a terror campaign with the aim of blowing up British and American installations in Egypt to undermine the progressively friendly ties expected from the impending new treaty removing the British military presence from Egypt. This attempt is now known as the infamous "Lavon Affair." It was not only directed at arousing British and American anger over the destruction of their facilities by "Egyptian duplicity," it would also demonstrate to the Anglo-American powers that Nasser was not firmly in command and could not control internal opposition.

Israel was concerned. (1) If Britain was no longer around to be the vent for Nasser's nationalism, he would likely turn it on Israel. (2) The British Suez base was a "blocking pad" for Egyptian military adventures eastward. Without it, Israel would be in the direct line of any Egyptian aspirations of territorial expansion in pan-Arabism.

The "Lavon Affair"

To block the success of the proposed Anglo-Egyptian treaty, the order was given in June, 1954, to have the two Israeli cell organizations in Egypt plant bombs in Western facilities and in Egypt's post offices, banks, and cinemas. Initially the Israeli operation was successful; then the operatives were presumably betrayed by a double agent. All participants known by the Israeli intelligence commander in Egypt, Avraham Seidenberg,[56] were "discovered" by the Egyptian counter intelligence, routinely beaten in the interrogation process, and punished. Two committed suicide; one (who is generally recognized to have been innocent) was found hanged in his apartment after interrogation; another killed himself a few hours before his scheduled execution at dawn. Two were hanged; two received life sentences; two fifteen-year sentences; and others received lesser punishment or were acquitted.

In summary, this Israeli intelligence operation was a tragic failure. The Massad (Israel's intelligence organization) has acquired a reputation of unexcelled brilliance (the Eichmann case, the 1967 Six-Day War, the Entebbe Rescue). But the Lavon Affair must surely rank as the nadir of Israeli intelligence operations. Golan seems to be convinced that the "network" members were betrayed from within the group. His research[57] points to the fatal mistake of hiring a double agent to command the operation in Egypt; the agent then betrayed the participants to the Egyptian authorities. This same individual then succeeded in "miraculously" returning to Israel as a hero for having "risked his life in a futile effort to save his saboteurs in Egypt."

The Lavon Affair produced political upheavals in Israel as a result of the controversy over who authorized the abortive action and who should receive the blame. Originally the focus was on whether or not Defense Minister Pinhas Lavon had authorized the operation. The Dori-Olshan investigation concluded it was impossible to know whether Lavon had given the order. Forced to resign at this time were Defense Minister Lavon, Head of Special Task Force of Military Intelligence Motke Ben-Tzur, and Head of Military Intelligence Benjamin Jibly. Later, Premier Moshe Sharett resigned.

When in 1960 Avraham Seidenberg was tried on charges of illegally possessing confidential government information and establishing contact with an enemy agent—a case not directly related to the 1954 Lavon Affair—evidence came to light that important documents of the 1954 case had been destroyed, and perjury involving forged documents had taken place in the Dori-Olshan investigation at that time. Pinhas Lavon then insisted that the government act to officially clear his name. This resulted in a major political feud between Lavon and Ben-Gurion.[58]

At the time Israel was experiencing this bitter internal feuding, the internal politics of the Soviet Union was also intensely involved in the Kremlin rivalry of choosing a successor to Stalin, who died on March 5, 1953. Khrushchev eventually defeated his rivals in the politically fluid situation of succession politics, which had an important effect upon Soviet Middle East policy. For better or for worse, Joseph Stalin had charted the course of the Soviet ship of state for almost thirty years, a period including the unprecedented slaughter of

World War II in which the very survival of Russia itself was, for a time, very much in doubt. His rule had been a combination of ruthless barbarity associated with a technological revolution. Stalin was once referred to as "Genghis Khan with a telephone."[59]

Soviet Domestic Politics After Stalin's Death

Toward the end of his life Stalin seemed to recapture some of his anti-Semitism of the past. To what extent this was exacerbated by his characteristic paranoia regarding the security of the state or, alternatively, by the pressures of *aliyah* from the new state of Israel is not clear. The famous "doctors trials," previously discussed, fit into the prevailing mood of his last days.

When Stalin died, his power was divided among the members of the top group of the Soviet elite. Georgi Malenkov assumed the premiership and became the First Secretary of the Communist party. Molotov, Bulganin, Kaganovich, and Beria became Deputy Premiers and each took charge of one aspect of vital state machinery such as foreign affairs, the armed forces, industrial production, and internal security.

Right after Stalin's death there were a few months of confusion—a pulling back from confrontation which seemed to confound some writers into calling it a peace offensive. Territorial claims against Turkey were dropped; the Nasser–Neguib government, which had previously been referred to as fascist and reactionary, was now given a more friendly hearing; diplomatic relations were re-established with Israel; rapprochment with Yugoslavia was pushed, etc. Georgi Malenkov, in a speech to the Supreme Soviet on August 8, 1953, broke with the Stalin tradition and, for the first time, made favorable references to the Arab governments in the Middle East. (Favorable comments were now also made about the third world governments of India and southeast Asia.)

It was under the Malenkov government that the beginning of a program of economic and political penetration into the Middle East was undertaken. Somewhat later, "military socialism" was discovered as potentially progressive; furthermore, the principle that only an industrial proletariat could create a successful progressive revolution was pushed aside by openness to the revolutionary potential of "bourgeoisie nationalists" in developing countries.

Shortly after Stalin's death, Nikita Khrushchev broke into the top ruling elite. Beria was arrested on June 26 on charges of plotting to seize power and was executed that same year. Malenkov's position began to erode in mid-1954 in a power struggle which was under the facade of the heavy industry versus consumer goods controversy. In fact, the rivalry between Malenkov and Khrushchev certainly included a personal struggle for power. Beginning in 1954 it became increasingly evident that Khrushchev's "platform," in maneuvering for power, advocated the priority of heavy industry. He criticized the Malenkov thesis that consumer goods should now receive the emphasis which the progress in heavy industry in the past made possible.

Malenkov, together with Soviet Foreign Minister Molotov, also favored a foreign policy of mutual nuclear deterrence with the West. Their policy area of emphasis was Europe. Challenging this was Khrushchev, Bulganin and the military who emphasized new directions involving a rapproachment with the third world and the nonaligned nations.

In 1954 the Soviets were satisfied to limit their efforts to probing the situation in several non-aligned countries. The Soviet leadership evaluated the circumstances of India, Afghanistan, Guatemala (to which the Soviets, through Czechoslovakia, had sent arms), Syria, and Egypt. The Soviet leadership also made steps to improve relations with China. Khrushchev visited that country in September, 1954, in what turned out to be a Soviet–Chinese summit meeting in which Khrushchev blamed the strained relations of the two countries on Molotov, the Soviet Foreign Minister. An attempt was made to improve relations with Yugoslavia in May, 1955, when Khrushchev visited Tito. The rapprochement with Yugoslavia was an integral part of Khrushchev's new initiatives in the Soviet Union's post-Stalin foreign policy. Neither Molotov nor Malenkov accompanied Khrushchev on his trips to China or to Yugoslavia. Khrushchev's contacts with Egypt were similarly not fully shared with Molotov. The latter was probably not aware of the initial stages of the Soviet–Egyptian entente taking place at the end of 1954.[60]

Khrushchev had previously, in coalition with Molotov, undermined the authority of Malenkov in a similar manner at the CPSU Plenum, January 25–31, 1955. However, now Khrushchev very clearly turned on Molotov and undermined his position at the CPSU Plenum in July, 1955—the occasion when he accused Molotov of obstructing Soviet–Yugoslavian relations. Khrushchev escalated the rivalry with Malenkov when he caused a commentary to be published, in the January 24, 1955, issue of *Pravda*, which was sharply critical of those who gave priority to consumer goods. On February 9, 1955, Malenkov felt forced to resign; he was succeeded by Bulganin as Premier. This set the stage for the Khrushchev–Bulganin visit to the third world states to the south in 1955.

A "New Look" in Soviet Middle East Policy

Beginning in the Malenkov period and increasing under Bulganin, Khrushchev was the new director of Soviet policy toward the Middle East and south Asia. An Egyptian trade mission was invited to Soviet-controlled eastern Europe in early 1954. This proved successful in that a number of barter agreements providing for the exporting of Egyptian cotton were effected. A Soviet cultural centre was opened in Cairo later that same year. The same new Soviet policy of economic and political penetration was directed toward the Indian subcontinent. This latter thrust culminated in the famous

November, 1955, visit of Khrushchev and Bulganin to India and her neighbors.

In February, 1956, at the 20th Congress of the Soviet Communist Party, Khrushchev conceptualized this new openness to nationalist movements in post-colonial states by abandoning the traditional Stalinist theory of the "two camps" (as mentioned previously), replacing it by the "two zones" model.

At this important meeting, resolutions were also passed which welcomed friendly relations with Egypt, Afghanistan, India and Burma. Egypt and Syria were explicitly mentioned as worthy of support since they were standing "on the side of Peace."[61]

In the broader perspective of Soviet policy, it was also at this occasion of the Twentieth Congress that Khrushchev delivered the famous "secret report" on Stalin's crimes. Khrushchev's attack on the very center of past Soviet policy facilitated the new policy directions toward third world states. Yet the attack on Stalin's "cult of the personality" foreshadowed new dangers as portrayed by Haynie (in *The Greensboro* (N. C.) *Daily News*). Below is the caricature of Nikita Khrushchev's de-Stalinization thrust depicted as letting the genie out of the bottle which might return to haunt the Kremlin leadership.

Important political decisions were also taking place in the United States and Great Britain which had their impact on the Middle East. Simultaneous with Khrushchev's maneuvering in the Kremlin, the new Republican administration in the White House moved into high gear to encourage the British to heal the breach with Egypt and re-establish relations on a stable treaty basis. In this context, success in the dispute over the Sudan was achieved in 1953, and the thorny issue of British troops in the Suez Canal Zone was resolved in 1954. The Russians were unhappy with Nasser about the treaty. They feared a stabilization of Western influence in the Middle East. This acted as a catalyst for Soviet involvement on the side of the Arabs when the opportunity arose.

'YOU SURE HE IS UNDER CONTROL?'

Naynle in The Greensboro (N C) Daily News

The Soviet Union regarded the Suez Agreement as directed against its own interests. The United States might still convince Nasser to join the proposed Baghdad Pact or other Islamic defense alliances. Nasser was anxious to develop an Arab collective security pact with Western arms.[62] The subject was discussed at the Arab League Council in December, 1954.[63]

I. Alexandrov reflected the critical Soviet attitude on the Suez agreement when he discussed it in *Pravda*, August 8, 1954:

... It seems that the present Anglo-Egyptian agreement on the Suez Canal zone does not guarantee Egypt territorial integrity, sovereignty, noninterference in its internal affairs, or equality in its relations with the Western countries .... In concluding the agreement, the Egyptian government is taking a dangerous step toward supporting American plans for a Middle East Command, a direct threat to the cause of peace in the Middle East.[64]

Alexandrov also denounced the United States' role in the Anglo-Egyptian agreement by referring to the United States as the "middleman" in bridging the gap between inherently different interests in the Middle East. Furthermore, he said, the United States "is demanding that Egypt firmly re-examine its position with respect to the Middle East command and is diligently imposing its enslaving 'aid' on Egypt."[65]

The Suez Agreement was a turning point in Moscow's thinking regarding the Middle East. The new Soviet leadership must have realized that a shift from the Stalinist "hard line" toward the Middle East was not enough in light of the Anglo-American activism in the area. "It may have appeared to Moscow that Nasser, despite his rhetoric about independence and Arab nationalism, was going to be a less effective anti-imperialist force than Farouk's ministers had been."[66] The Suez agreement revived Moscow's suspicion of Nasser's "progressive" regime. Moscow was also aware of Nasser's harrassment of the Egyptian Communists.

Soviet policy makers came to the conclusion that the Suez Agreement was the beginning of a new United States–British diplomatic offensive in the Middle East; counter-measures by the Soviet Union seemed to be increasingly urgent. To counter this Western pressure, the Soviets became convinced that more would be required than its cooling of friendship with Israel to stop Western diplomatic efforts seeking to bring a Middle East containment alliance to fruition (the Russians considered it "capitalist encirclement"). It was the United States which was leading the Western initiative. Already the foundation was being built through bi-lateral understandings and unilateral pledges of aid.

Moscow made the decision to take determined counter-measures. This urgent nature of Soviet opposition to the impending Baghdad Pact was the beginning of the Soviet-Egyptian entente, a drastic step in the Soviet policy switch from pro-Israel to pro-Arab. The new policy was symbolically "signed, sealed, and delivered" by the "Czech arms deal" with Egypt, announced in September, 1955.

The West's proposed Middle East Defense Organization urging the Middle East to join the Western bloc in the bi-polar confrontation was, therefore, the single most important factor leading to the pro-Arab policy of the Soviet Union. We shall discuss later the role this proposed organization played in Soviet domestic politics and the power struggle within the Kremlin.

The Dulles Middle East Policy

In 1954 while the British, with American encouragement, were negotiating with Nasser to restore relations on a firm treaty basis—a process which bore fruit in the Anglo-Egyptian Treaty of October, 1954—Dulles pushed ahead with two issues which figured very importantly as roadblocks to future friendly relations with Egypt. The first was the Arab–Israeli dispute. From 1954–1956 there were sustained efforts to find a solution to this difficulty in American–Egyptian relations. Nasser emphasized the difficulty of accepting a Jewish state which physically divided the Arab world. Israel's successful territorial aggrandizement of a continuous land connection to Elath on the Gulf of Aqaba had eliminated a very crucial land connection between Egypt and the Arab East. The State Department, under Dulles' initiative, hoped to solve Nasser's complaint pragmatically by working out a very elaborate, technical masterpiece. Mohammed Hassanein Heikal captured the humorous dimension of the American proposal to provide "sovereign land bridges" to both Israel and the Arabs over the same land area.

Heikal relates how the Americans, well known for their ingrained optimism about the ability of their technical know-how to solve the world's problems, proposed to Nasser a "geometric solution" to the territorial separation of the Arab world by the Israeli Negev. The American plan would give to Egypt and Jordan just enough of a triangular wedge of the Negev to make an Arab road possible, meeting at a point on the Israeli highway to Elath.

> The crux of the plan was that the Americans would build a complicated overpass system by which the Israelis would use an underpass connecting them with Elath while Egypt and Jordan would be connected by an overpass built over the Israeli road.
>
> The Americans put an enormous amount of work on the scheme. The United States Army, the CIA, and the State Department produced dozens of detailed engineering drawings for building this overpass in the desert. These drawings were shown to Nasser who examined them with interest and then destroyed the whole scheme. "The Arabs," he said, "will be on the overpass and the Israelis will be on the underpass. Well, all right, suppose an Arab on the overpass one day felt the call of nature and it landed on an Israeli car on the underpass . . . What would happen? There would be a war."
>
> Nasser always referred to that meeting as the "pee-pee discussion." He felt that the Americans were too concerned with superficial and artificial ways of settling problems, and he could not take these gimmicks seriously.[67]

A second obstacle to the development of friendly relations with Nasser's Egypt was the American effort to create a Middle East defense organization. Nasser was simply not receptive to cooperation with the West in a joint defense arrangement directed against Soviet Communist expansion. He protested to Dulles that (1) collective defense in the Arab world should be the responsibility of the Arab League, (2) the greatest danger of Communism was from within, not from without, and (3) Egypt had a leadership role to play in the Arab world—the implication being that any U.S. attempt to bypass Egypt to negotiate with arch-rival Iraq as leader of the Arab world in the Middle East defense organization would be considered a serious threat to Egypt's regional aspirations. Dulles made the fateful decision to confront Egypt on this last point. Egypt would be by passed for Iraq. To Washington there appeared to be no alternative if the regional defense arrangement were to be built.

Turkey's precondition for joining a Middle East defense alliance had been met by agreeing to its membership in NATO (1952). The initial steps in creating the organization were taken in February, 1954, when Turkey and Pakistan (which was interested in Western arms in its confrontation with India) announced their intent of closer collaboration for mutual defense. A few days later, the United States publicly announced its intention of granting economic and military aid to Pakistan. Both Egypt and India raised objections, with the former reaffirming its intent to frustrate U.S. efforts in the Arab world. The Soviet Union sent protests to both Pakistan and Turkey.

In spite of the diplomatic protests, Turkey and Pakistan went ahead and formally concluded a joint defense agreement on April 2, 1954. To a discerning observer, the strong feeling of opposition on the part of both Egypt and the USSR was foreboding not only to Washington's plans for the area, but also from the perspective of Jerusalem which was very apprehensive about the resulting commonality of interests between Moscow and Cairo. Pushing Moscow and Cairo into a new alignment of forces in the Middle East would create major problems for Israel's national security. From the early 1950s when, after the Korean invasion, the United States began pushing for a containment alliance in the Middle East, Israel realized the dilemma it faced. The Arabs would never be willing to join an alliance which included Israel; yet the organization would be the means whereby the Arabs would receive weapons which then might be used against Israel. In fact, Israel was never invited to join the Middle East defense pact.

On May 19, 1954, the United States and Pakistan signed a defense agreement which cleared the way for American arms shipments to that country. An agreement was also reached with Iraq to receive Western arms. In spite of the traditional Iraqi–Egypt rivalry, in late summer of 1954 Premier Nuri es Said of Iraq approached Egypt about participating in the proposed regional collective security alliance. These events were taking place simultaneously with the British–Egyptian negotiations on the termination of the British military presence at Suez.

Iraq's efforts to include Egypt ended in failure. Consequently, Iraq decided to go ahead, in spite of sharp criticism from Cairo, with the "Northern Tier" defense alliance which came into being under the name of the Baghdad Pact, with Iraq and Turkey signing the Treaty of Mutual Cooperation at Baghdad on February 24, 1955.

Egypt (and to some degree Saudi Arabia and Syria) immediately moved into strong opposition to keep other members of the Arab League from accepting Western invitations to join. Great Britain joined the Baghdad Pact in April, Pakistan in September, and Iran in October (1955). France and the United States never joined; although the latter was the primary force behind the Pact's creation and its maintenance— which included being the primary supplier of arms.

Iraq's access to Western arms, plus the advantages of leadership in a Western-supported regional defense alliance, tipped the balance in its favor in the Baghdad–Cairo rivalry. To counter Iraq's moves, Nasser also requested Western arms and took the initiative in seeking to organize a rival defense alliance of Arab states. To Nasser's bitter disappointment, both efforts failed. He refused to accept the Western condition for arms aid, namely, that the arms could only be used for internal security and defense. Furthermore, Lebanon and Jordan refused to join with Egypt against Iraq. Only Syria (and to some degree Saudi Arabia) supported Nasser in these efforts.

Syria's Role in the Soviet Pro-Arab Policy

Not only Egypt, but also Syria, played a role in the Soviet Union's switch to the Arabs' side. Even though Moscow was cool toward the Arabs in the early post-war years, Syria enjoyed a slight Soviet preference in relations with Arab states due to its relatively active Communist party and its front organizations. Furthermore, Syrians played an historic leadership role in the Arab nationalist movement. The Soviet favoritism for Syria could also be explained by the enduring qualities of one of the Arab world's most effective Communist party leaders, Khalid Bakdash, an ethnic Kurd. Kurds were (and still are) usually found among the economically deprived of the socioeconomic classes of Syria. Historically, the Communist movement seemed to be more appealing to this deprived group; in any case, after World War II approximately one-third of the Syrian Communist party membership was Kurdish. The popular Kurd, Khalid Bakdash, became first secretary of the Syrian Communist Party in 1934, and he was still the major Communist leader during the crucial events of 1955–58.

A rise in Soviet affinity toward Syria occurred after the fall of the Adib Shishakli dictatorship in February of 1954. The major political struggle in Syria continued to be waged in the army between those factions (1) supporting the Baathists who tended to be anti-Western and favored cooperation with Egypt and Saudi Arabia against the Hashimite rulers of Iraq and Jordan, and (2) those supporting the Syrian Social Nationalist Party (the party of Shishakli) which was strongly anti-Communist. The SSNP favored a Syrian policy of identity with the Fertile Crescent states as opposed to Egypt and was more favorably disposed to the West—although not at the expense of Syrian national sovereignty. The Syrian Communist

Party reaped a bonus in power and prestige by cooperating effectively with the Baathists in essentially liquidating the Syrian Social Nationalist Party after the latter was accused of conspiracy in the assassination of the Syrian Deputy Chief of Staff, Colonel Adnan Malki, in April, 1955.

The Syrian Communists, as was to be expected, served as a medium for increased Syrian affinity with Moscow. The Communists also voiced strong opposition to the Baghdad Pact. Later the Syrian Communist Party supported the government's action in seeking economic and military aid from the Soviet Union and in recognizing the People's Republic of China in November, 1956. Following Egypt's lead, Syria received, in 1956, Soviet military aid in excess of fifty million dollars. Syria's head of state made an official state visit to Moscow in the fall (1956) at the time of the Suez crisis. The momentum of increasing orientation toward Moscow continued until even the Baathists became alarmed to the point that they felt compelled to beg Nasser for a merger with Egypt to head off what many of them believed would become a Communist dominated government in Damascus.

The Baghdad Pact: Shock Waves in the Middle East

To return to the events of the Baghdad Pact, it was clear that Nasser considered Iraq to have betrayed the cause of Arab solidarity and neutrality. Iraq, furthermore, was openly challenging Egypt's leadership in the Arab World. On January 16, 1955, Salah Salem, the Egyptian Minister of National Guidance, in a press conference contended that Egypt "would pursue an independent foreign policy . . . and this requires the strengthening of the entity of the Arab League and the acquiescence of all its members to a united and independent foreign policy. . . ."[68] Although most of Salem's press conference was for local consumption, some of it was directed to the Soviet leadership as a confirmation of Egypt's attitude toward the Baghdad Pact. Moreover, Iraq's joining the Pact was considered as breaking the ranks of Arab solidarity and making a separate deal with the West; Cairo saw it as a deliberate Western move to punish Nasser and reward Nuri al-Said of Iraq for his cooperation. It was the United States using the historical "bi-polar" Fertile Crescent rivalry between Egypt and Iraq to further American (Western) interests. *Al-Ahram*, the Egyptian newspaper which unofficially represents government policy, pointed out the Soviet attitude vis-à-vis the Baghdad Pact:

> If the Turkish–Iraqi Pact would be against the Arab League . . . the strongest opposition would come from the Soviet Union because it considers the enforcement of the defense of the Middle East to be against its own interests and influence. . . .[69]

From the Soviet point of view, the Iraqi announcement of joining the northern tier defense was a setback in Soviet strategy in the Middle East, a more severe setback than the Suez Agreement. The Soviet press, under the by-line of Y. Bochkaryov, channeled its anti-Pact propaganda into a focus on renewed Western colonialism in the Middle East:

> . . . The armed forces of the Middle East members of the Baghdad Pact, have, in large measure, lost their national countenance and are gradually being turned into an appendage to the U.S.–British military machine. And this means that the armed forces of Turkey, Pakistan, Iran and Iraq, instead of being the mainstay of national independence, are being turned into instruments of Western aggressive policy. The real nature of the Baghdad Pact can be gauged also from its direct tie-up with such aggressive military organizations as NATO in Europe and SEATO in Southeast Asia.[70]

On February 8, 1955, V. M. Molotov, the Soviet Foreign Minister, delivered a major foreign policy report to the Supreme Soviet. Molotov made several references to the Middle East:

> We cannot say that the national-liberation movement in the Arab East, for example, has attained the power and scope which distinguish that movement in a number of Asian countries. The

countries in this area, especially those which possess substantial oil deposits, are still painfully dependent on so-called "Western" countries, which have seized control of their oil and other natural resources. It also happens in these parts that governments are formed and deposed at the will of American and British oil companies or other foreign capitalist concerns. But the national-liberation movement in this area is steadily growing nonetheless.[71]

More specifically, Molotov criticized the Iraqi government in light of the impending Baghdad Pact. He asserted that "the fact that Iraq has broken off relations with the USSR is chiefly to be attributed to the over-eagerness of the present Iraq government to dance to the tune of the 'Western' imperialists."[72] He continued, however, by favorable references to the Arab states:

> ... It is presumably known in the Arab countries that the people of the USSR entertain friendly feelings for them, and that in the Soviet Union they have had and will have, a reliable support in the defense of their sovereignty and national independence. . . ."[73]

Contradictory thrusts such as those exemplified by this speech are not foreign to Soviet pronouncements; one can see the same pattern in Gromyko's statements at the UN in 1948. However, the foreign policy statement by Molotov on February 8, 1955, tended to reveal the divergent policy positions of leadership rivalry in the top inner circle of government. It reflected the behind-the-scenes squabbles over policy toward the Middle East as Professor Ra'anan indicates:

> It is hardly likely to be a mere coincidence that the Molotov–Khrushchev dispute over Near Eastern (and other) issues can be placed, with some assurance, at a point midway between the January plenum and the elevation of Bulganin to the premiership namely, during the first week of February, 1955.[74]

Ra'anan explained the contradiction in Molotov's statement by suggesting that the Khrushchev faction might have insisted on a few alterations just prior to the delivery of the statement to the Supreme Soviet on February 8, 1955.[75] After the presentation of the statement, the Soviet press played down the unfavorable statements regarding the Middle East. As a matter of fact, when *Al-Ahram* reported the summary of Molotov's foreign policy statement it did not mention the unfavorable references regarding the Arab states, but mentioned only general comments regarding the liberation movement in Africa and Asia.[76]

Foreign Minister Molotov was not aware of the degree of growing intimacy between Cairo and Moscow, since Khrushchev was in control of most of Molotov's functions and the discussions between the Egyptian and the Soviet governments were conducted by the intelligence services of both countries.[77]

Presumably Molotov was not even aware of the Soviet–Egyptian contacts in Ankara in January, 1955.[78] However, by the first week of February, 1955, Molotov could not have been ignorant of what was going on between Moscow and Cairo, especially after the Soviet government had asked the government of Czechoslovakia to send its "trade" delegation to Cairo. As indicated by Ra'anan, "It was precisely at this moment that the power balance in the Kremlin shifted."[79] Molotov went ahead to deliver his foreign policy statement on February 8, 1955, on the assumption that the Soviet–Egyptian interest convergence would be a temporary phenomenon.

NOTES

1. *New York Times*, January 10, 1952, p. 12.
2. *Jerusalem Post*, January 17, 1951, p. 1
3. *New York Times*, January 30, 1951, p. 5.
4. Ibid., January 31, 1951, p. 5.
5. Ibid.
6. Ibid.
7. Karmi Shweitzer, "Soviet Policy Towards Israel, 1946–1952," *Mizan*, XI (January–February, 1969), p. 25.
8. Avigdor Dagan, *Moscow and Jerusalem* (New York: Abelard–Schuman, 1970), p. 57.
9. *Jerusalem Post*, October 18, 1951, p. 1.
10. Ibid., November 22, 1951, p. 1.
11. Ibid., February 28, 1952, p. 1.
12. Ibid., December 24, 1951, p. 1.
13. Ibid., November 25, 1952, p. 3.
14. As quoted by the *Jerusalem Post*, November 24, 1952, p. 1.
15. Foreign Radio Broadcasts, *Daily Report*, No. 235, December 2, 1952, p. 1.
16. Shweitzer, p. 26.
17. Ibid.
18. *Jerusalem Post*, January 14, 1953, p. 1.
19. Ibid.
20. V. Minayev, "Zionist Agents of the American Secret Service," *New Times*, No. 4 (January, 1953), pp. 15–16.
21. *Jerusalem Post*, January 20, 1953, p. 1.
22. Ibid., February 10, 1953, p. 1.
23. Ibid., February 11, 1953, p. 3.
24. Ibid.
25. Ibid., February 13, 1953, p. 1.
26. Ibid.
27. Shweitzer, p. 26.
28. *Imperialisticheskaia borka za Afriku i Osvoboditelnoe Dvizhenie Narodov* (Moscow, 1953), p. 126.
29. Ibid., 1954, p. 97ff.
30. I. I. Potekhin and Olderogge, eds. *Narody Afriki* (Moscow, 1954), p. 213.
31. G. M. Malenkov, "The International Situation and the Foreign Policy of the Soviet Union," *Supplement to New Times*, No. 33 (August, 1953), pp. 14–15.
32. Ibid., p. 15.
33. United Nations Security Council, *Official Records, Eighth Year, Sup-*

plement for October, November and December 1953, Document S/3151/Rev. 2, pp. 79–80.

34. United Nations Security Council, *Official Records, 656th Meeting*, 22 January 1954, pp. 6–9.

35. Ibid., p. 29.

36. Ibid., p. 28.

37. United Nations Security Council, *Official Records, Supplement for January, February and March 1954*, p. 44.

38. United Nations Security Council, *Official Records, 664th Meeting*, 29 March 1954, p. 17.

39. *Jerusalem Post*, March 31, 1954, p. 4.

40. Foreign Radio Broadcasts, *Daily Report*, No. 63, April 1, 1954, p. 1.

41. *Jerusalem Post*, March 31, 1954, p. 4.

42. Ibid., March 24, 1954, p. 1.

43. U.S., Congress, House, Committee on Foreign Affairs, *Mutual Security Act of 1954*, Hearing, 83rd Cong., 2nd Sess., April 13, 1954 (Washington: Government Printing Office, 1954), p. 204.

44. Ibid., p. 473.

45. Ibid.

46. Karmi Shweitzer, "Soviet Policy Towards Israel, 1953–1956," *Mizan*, XI (May–June, 1969), p. 176.

47. *Jerusalem Post*, May 11, 1954, p. 1.

48. Ibid., p. 2.

49. Mohammed Hassanein Heikal, *The Cairo Documents* (Garden City, New York: Doubleday & Co., 1973), p. 43.

50. Ibid.

51. Foreign Radio Broadcasts, *Daily Report*, No. 235.

52. Ibid.

53. *Jerusalem Post*, August 31, 1954, p. 2.

54. Ibid., p. 1.

55. Ibid., September 2, 1954, p. 1.

56. Aviezer Golan, *Operation Susannah* (New York: Harper & Row, 1978), pp. 42, 47. According to the author, Mazza, Farhi, and Damon "were the only three members of the network who did not fall into the hands of the Egyptian counterintelligence" (p. 47). These three, it should be noted, were never introduced to Avraham Seidenberg.

57. See Golan, pp. 42, 47, 60, 63–64, 80, 89–90, 283–88, and 376. Golan (p. 80) affirms the fact that the Israeli intelligence community concluded that the Jewish group in Egypt had been betrayed by a double agent. In 1957 (p. 285) Seidenberg violated his orders and contacted Nuri Otman in Germany, who was now the Egyptian military attaché in West Germany but who had been, in 1954, deputy commander of Egypt's military intelligence and head of the Egyptian army's security service. In 1954 he had also been directly in charge of investigating the "Zionist network" in Egypt.

When the imprisoned members of the Israeli network in Egypt were traded for captured Egyptian troops after the Six-Day War, the group went to see David Ben Gurion at Sdeh Boker. The former premier said they had been "sold" (betrayed) (p. 376).

58. For additional information, see: Aviezer Golan, *Operation Susannah* (New York: Harper & Row, 1978). "The 'Lavon Affair,' " *Encyclopedia Judaica*, X, 1971, 1478–79. *Time*, Nov. 7, 1960, pp. 37–38. *New York Times*, Oct. 8, 1960, p. 6; Dec. 26, 1960, p. 4; Jan. 13, 1961, p. 4; Jan. 21, 1961, p. 2; Jan. 22, 1961, Part IV, p. 8; Feb. 4, 1961, p. 6.

59. David Dallin, *From Purge to Coexistence* (Chicago: Henry Regnery Co., 1964), p. 173.

60. Uri Ra'anan, *The USSR Arms the Third World* (Cambridge, Mass.: The MIT Press, 1969), pp. 88–90.

61. Translated from *Pravda*, February 18, 1956.

62. Keith Wheelock, *Nasser's New Egypt* (New York: Frederick A. Praeger, 1960), p. 220.

63. Ibid.

64. *Pravda*, August 8, 1954, p. 4, as cited in the *Current Digest of the Soviet Press*, VI, No. 32, September 22, 1954, p. 18.

65. Ibid., p. 17.

66. A. S. Becker and A. L. Horelick, *Soviet Policy in the Middle East* (R-504-FF) (Santa Monica, Cal.: Rand Corporation, 1970), p. 21.

67. Heikal, p. 56.

68. *Al-Ahram*, January 17, 1955, p. 1.

69. Ibid., January 14, 1955, p. 1.

70. Y. Bochkaryov, "Pact of Agression," *New Times*, No. 50 (December, 1955), p. 18.

71. V. M. Molotov, "The International Situation and the Foreign Policy of the Soviet Government," *New Times*, No. 7 (February, 1955), p. 13.

72. Ibid., pp. 22–23.

73. Ibid., p. 23.

74. Ra'anan, p. 121.

75. Ibid., p. 103.

76. *Al-Ahram*, February 9, 1955, p. 5.

77. Ra'anan, p. 119.

78. Ibid., p. 72.

79. Ibid., p. 119.

CHAPTER 9

Baghdad Pact Politics: Moscow Sides with the Arabs Against Israel

On February 24, 1955, the so-called Baghdad Pact came into being with Iraq and Turkey entering into the bi-lateral agreement officially known as the Pact of Mutual Cooperation. The Pact was consummated through the initiative of the United States which bankrolled and provided the military equipment, yet it never officially became a member. Plans called for other Arab states to join but, when Nasser proved successful in organizing the street mob in Jordan against it, no other Arab state joined. The role the Baghdad Pact played in influencing Soviet Middle East policy is elaborated later.

The Gaza Raid

Another event of importance in 1955 was Israel's strong retaliatory raid against the Egyptian army outpost in Gaza. On February 28, 1955, Israel, under Ben Gurion's leadership, sent a military force into Gaza "to teach the Arabs a lesson." The strike against Egypt in Gaza reflected the "hard line" orientation of Ben Gurion,[1] who had only two weeks before succeeded Pinhas Lavon as Minister of Defense when the latter resigned due to accusations stemming from the infamous "Lavon Affair." The humiliation of Egypt's military forces by Israel in the Gaza attack was an important factor in causing Nasser urgently to turn to the Soviet Union for weapons. Moscow was shocked to realize the military weakness of Egypt. This incident gave the Soviets another opportunity to denounce

Israel and support Egypt diplomatically at the United Nations. The Soviet delegate, A. A. Sobolov, declared in the Security Council:

> The circumstances of the Gaza incident also show that Israel was responsible for it. Obviously these acts by the Israel armed forces are a serious violation of the United Nations Charter and are increasing tension in the area. The Security Council consequently cannot ignore this state of affairs.[2]

French Support for Israel

At this point the increasing French support of Israel became a factor in the Middle East situation of increasing Soviet–Egyptian commonality against Israel. The French de facto violation of their commitment under the Tripartite Declaration of 1950 came about as a result of the determination to punish Egypt for supporting France's enemy in the Algerian war. Mohammed Hassanein Heikal, claiming to present the Egyptian perspective, said the Egyptian Intelligence Service found out about the French shipment of arms, dating from 1954, after the Israeli Gaza raid. Heikal claims Nasser began his active support of Algerian rebels *after*, rather than *before*, the French sent arms to Israel. Nasser's strategy, according to Heikal, was to keep the French occupied with their arms in Algeria so none would be available to send to Israel.[3] The credibility of Heikal's statements can be challenged.

Nasser's Quest for Arms

It is conceivable that if the Soviet's GRU had not known about the Israeli purchases of arms from France, the Egyptians would have told them, in view of the situation in the Middle East and Egypt's growing desire to obtain arms from any source including the United States. In February, 1955, Nasser asked Henry Byroade, the U.S. Ambassador to Egypt, about the possibility of obtaining heavy armaments from the United States. Ambassador Byroade checked with Washington about this. Dulles demurred; he was unhappy with Nasser's intention to attend the Bandung Conference of Afro-Asian States scheduled to convene on April 18, 1955. Ra'anan pointed out that "it is unlikely that the Egyptian leader would have approached Washington at this delicate stage (February–March, 1955) without first explaining his motives to Moscow."[4] Most probably Nasser wanted to ease the expected strong Western reaction to the "thunderbolt" of Egypt's arms deal with the Soviets when it became public knowledge.

Premier Nasser felt it necessary to present Egypt's position with regard to the Baghdad Pact in a major foreign policy speech on March 31, 1955.[5] The defense of the Middle East, he said, should emanate from the area itself, from the Arab countries and not from foreign states and foreign domination, including Communist domination. However, in the same speech Nasser indicated that ". . . the West regarded this behavior to be against its own interest which is the encirclement of the Soviet Union."[6]

The speech was intended by Nasser to communicate Egyptian foreign policy messages to both the Soviet Union and the United States. The Soviets, Nasser calculated, would react favorably to his opposition to Western "encirclement" of the Soviet Union. On the other hand, the refusal to accept "Communist domination" would please Washington and keep the door open for the ongoing arms negotiations with the United States in case the negotiations with the Soviets failed. Nasser was astute enough to know that a statement of intentions— especially since the arms proposal followed a circuitous route via Prague—was no guarantee that the arms would ever physically arrive in Egypt.

Nasser's speech was targeted for additional objectives. By re-affirming Egypt's opposition to any Western Middle East containment alliance directed against the Soviet Union, he strengthened Khrushchev's hand in the Kremlin decision-making process for favorable action on the secretly proposed arms shipment to Egypt.

Moscow Woos the Arabs

On April 16, 1955, the USSR Ministry of Foreign Affairs released a statement on the Middle East. It reflected Soviet antagonism to the Baghdad Pact[7] and a renewed determination to counter the Western efforts by encouraging Arab antagonism, and to invite the opposing Arab governments to join the Soviet Union in common opposition to the renewed Western involvement in the Middle East. It would give states like Egypt a new policy option.

Note the following portion of the Soviet communique:

> The situation in the Near and Middle East has recently deteriorated considerably, owing to the new attempts by certain Western powers to involve the Near and Middle Eastern countries in military groupings meant to serve as adjuncts to the aggressive North Atlantic bloc. . . .

> It goes without saying that the Soviet Union cannot be indifferent to the situation taking shape in the Near and Middle East, since the formation of blocs and the creation of foreign military bases in Near and Middle Eastern countries have a direct bearing on the security of the USSR. The Soviet goverment's position should be all the more understandable because the USSR is situated in close proximity to these countries, which cannot be said of other foreign powers, such as the U.S.A., which is thousands of kilometers away from this area. Non-participation by Near and Middle Eastern countries in aggressive military blocs would be an important prerequisite for ensuring their security and the best guarantee against their involvement in dangerous military adventures.[8]

The British press noted that the Soviet statement was timed for release just prior to the Bandung Conference of April, 1955. The Soviet government coordinated the statement with its efforts to promote Nasser's image as a world class leader of the third world at the Afro-Asian conference in Indonesia. The statement suggested future possibilities for a growing affinity between the Soviet Union and the Egyptian-led Arab states.

Other Arab states responded with enthusiasm to the April 16 Soviet policy statement. On April 23 Farid el-Khani, Syrian Envoy Extraordinary and Minister Plenipotentiary to the Soviet Union, expressed the gratitude of the Syrian government for the pro-Arab position taken by the Union of Soviet Socialistic Republics. Farid el-Khani's statement was given a very favorable notice in *Pravda*:

> . . . The Syrian government expressed gratitude to the Soviet government in this delicate situation for the interest and attention it is showing in Near and Middle Eastern events and for the intention expressed by the Soviet government to refer this matter to the U.N. if the Western powers continue their pressure.[9]

Iran, Turkey, and Iraq opposed the Soviet Ministry of Foreign Affairs statement. Iraq considered the statement incompatible with the reality of the situation in the Middle East;[10] Iran criticized the Soviet memo as a form of unacceptable Soviet pressure on its foreign policy;[11] while the Turkish press considered it as an attempt to obstruct the Middle East Defense Pact.[12]

In May, 1955, the Soviets elaborated their newly established posture toward Egypt and the Arab states under Western pressure to join the Pact. N. A. Bulganin, in a speech at the Warsaw Conference, May 11–14, 1955, explained Soviet foreign policy toward the Middle East:

> We know that strong pressure is being brought to bear on a number of Near and Middle East states to compel them to join military blocs which are being formed as adjuncts to the aggressive North-Atlantic alliance. Pressure is being exerted on Syria, Egypt and other Arab countries, and also on the Soviet Union's neighbour, Afghanistan.

Referring to the Soviet statement of April 16, 1955, concerning the Middle East, he stated:

> In connection with the growing tension in the Near and Middle East, the Soviet government, in its recent statement on the security of the area, emphasized that it cannot remain indifferent to the situation developing there. The Soviet government declared that if the policy of pressure and threats in relation to the Near and Middle East countries is persisted in, this question will have to be examined by the United Nations.[13]

By referring to the United Nations, the Soviet Union would be in a better diplomatic position to retreat if Western reaction to the arms deal were too forceful.

The Bandung Conference

As revealed by Heikal, when Nasser met Chou En-lai in Rangoon on their way to the Bandung Conference of April 18, 1955, Premier Nasser expressed his desire to obtain arms from the Soviet Union. He told Chou En-lai that Moscow's attitude toward Arab nationalist leaders had changed drastically. Earlier the Soviets were very suspicious of them, considering them a group of fascists suppressing the masses. Recently, however, as a result of Egypt's opposition "to imperialism and the Baghdad Pact, which was aimed at the Soviet Union," the Soviet Union had turned to friendly and supportive relations with Egypt.[14]

Chou En-lai supported the Khrushchev position toward third world states and sought to help him in the behind-the-scenes power struggle with Molotov now going on in the Kremlin. The Chinese leaders were favorably disposed to playing an intermediary role between Nasser and Khrushchev. They were also willing to promote Nasser's stature at the Bandung Conference. The Soviet Union did not participate directly in the Bandung Conference, but voiced its approval of the principles affirmed by the participants.

The Soviet Arms Deal with Nasser

Discussions regarding the arms deal continued in Cairo during May, June, and July, 1955, between Daniel Solod, the Soviet Ambassador in Cairo, and Premier Nasser.[15] Also representing the Soviet side was Colonel Nimoshenko, the Soviet military attaché in Cairo, while the Egyptian side was represented by Ali Sabri and Hafez Ismail. The Soviet Union wanted the talks to remain secret in light of the upcoming Geneva summit conference. As put by Heikal, "The Russians felt that if they supplied arms openly, it would be taken as a deliberate breach of the spirit of Geneva."[16]

By July, 1955, it was clear that the Khrushchev faction had won the fight. Molotov's position was undermined at the July 4, 1955, Plenum of the CPSU Central Committee. The Soviet leadership, after the July Plenum, went to Geneva to attend the summit meeting which was given considerable importance by the Soviet government in terms of its new directions in Soviet security strategy. The Soviet Union showed some flexibility at the meeting. While the summit meeting was going on, Khrushchev sent Dimitri Shepilov to Cairo for an appraisal of Western intentions and their probable counterbalance to the impending arms deal. Shepilov successfully wrapped up the technicalities of the arms deal, and the arms began arriving in Egypt in August, 1955.

Soviet behavior was almost predictable after the Geneva summit meeting. A year earlier Henry Byroade had stated:

> It has been my view that the Middle East, on the timetable of the Soviet Union, has been placed in priority behind that of Europe and the Far East simply because they look upon it as an area that can wait. The more Russia's aggressive moves are stalemated in Europe and the Far East, the more the danger grows for the Middle East.[17]

In fact, there were even more important factors than Byroade's conclusions. An explanation of the Soviet "bombshell" of supplying arms to Egypt must include even more important variables. Neither Nasser nor Khrushchev could politically afford to take the gamble until each had established his dominance in the national leadership rivalry (as well as coping with foreign threats). As already noted, Khrushchev achieved this by July, 1955. Nasser consolidated his effective national leadership in late 1954. In October he won British agreement to remove their military presence within 20 months. In November (1954) a certain Mahmoud Abdul Latif (charged with being a member of the Muslim Brotherhood) attempted to assassinate Nasser. The incident was used by the latter to remove his rival, General Mohammed Naguib, from the Presidency and place him under house arrest.

Another event which is thought to have contributed to the final Soviet decision to go ahead with the arms shipment to Egypt was the Israeli election of the third Knesset on July 26, 1955.

Results from this crucial election added to Egypt's concerns. The "hard line" Herut party almost doubled its representation in the Knesset by polling 13.25 per cent of the vote; while Mapai, the largest party, received only 32 per cent. Herut, representing the remains of the terrorist Irgun Zvai Leumi, emerged as the second largest party in Israel with fifteen seats in the Knesset.[18] The Arabs were apprehensive about the revival of an expansionist Israeli ideology along the lines of *Eretz Israel*. Although the Communist party gained one more seat, the Soviets were more concerned about the possible hard line trends in Israeli relations with the Arabs. Having sided with Egypt, the Soviet Union would have to show some support for its client state if threats to its security arose. This was another incentive for carrying through on the arms deal.

The arms deal with Czechoslovakia was announced publicly on September 27, 1955. It reflected the new direction of Soviet policy toward the Middle East after the death of Stalin. From Nasser's Egyptian perspective, accepting Communist arms (even though outlawing the Egyptian Communist Party) is explained by (1) Nasser's desire to get revenge against the

The September, 1955, Soviet arranged arms shipment to Egypt was viewed with alarm in the West. Knott, in The Dallas News, *portrays the destabilizing image of the event by showing it as upsetting the Middle East balance of power.*

Western powers who refused to give him arms, and (2) Nasser's anger at being bypassed by the West in favor of arch rival Iraq in the Baghdad Pact.

On September 29, 1955, Israel asked the Soviet Union for clarification regarding the arms deal. Moshe Sharett, Israeli

Prime Minister and Foreign Minister, met with Soviet Chargé d'Affaires M. Nikolai Klimov, and pointed out that the announcement of the arms deal by Nasser was contrary to what Israel was told when Israeli Ambassador to Moscow, Yosef Avidar, met A. Zaitzev, Director of the Near and Middle East Department at the Soviet Foreign Ministry, earlier in September, 1955.[19] On September 12, 1955, Zaitzev had informed the Israeli Ambassador Avidar that the Soviet Union had no knowledge of weapon sales to the Arab states or any transaction between the People's Democracies and the Arabs.[20] Commenting on the Soviet arms deal to Egypt, which created new security threats for Israel, Moshe Sharett said it represented "strong contradictions to the proclaimed policy of the Soviet Union in behalf of peace and reduction of armaments elsewhere throughout the world."[21] Sharett was referring to the Geneva talks on reduction of armaments attended by the Soviet Union and the Western Powers in July, 1955.

The Israeli Press in the meantime blasted the Israeli Government on foreign policy failures regarding the arms deal. *Lamerhav* (Ahdut Aa'avoda) attacked the Israeli foreign ministry for "having been instrumental in bringing about Israel's isolation in the international sphere causing setback upon setback."[22] *Davar* (Histadrut) stated that the Czechoslovak arms deal was "only a means of extorting concessions from the West for in reality it is Western arms that the Arabs want."[23] *Kol Ha'am* (Communist) mentioned Israel's vote on the Algerian question as a good example of what was wrong with the government's foreign policy. It pointed out that Israel's foreign policy "always sticks with the West despite the fact that Algeria deserves self-determination." "Unless there is a basic change," said *Kol Ha'am*, "this isolation, fraught with extreme danger, is bound to persist."[24]

On October 3, 1955, the Israeli Cabinet issued the following official communiqué:

At an extraordinary session yesterday the Cabinet heard a detailed review of the Prime Minister and Minister for Foreign Af-

fairs on the chain of events connected with the supplying of arms
to Egypt and on the steps that have been taken with the powers to
prevent an arms race and to defend Israel's security."[25]

The Israeli position regarding the arms deal was made
clearer by Moshe Sharett, the Israeli Prime Minister, in a
speech opening the foreign policy discussions in the Knesset
on October 18, 1955. Sharett said a defense pact was no substi-
tute for armaments, but he did not rule out the possibility of
some form of defense pact for Israel. Sharett also commented
specifically on Soviet behavior, asking rhetorically how the
Soviet initiative in the troubled Middle East contributed to
the world peace and stability which the Soviets proclaim they
seek.[26]

The debate in the Knesset on Sharett's speech followed the
pattern of party alignment. Menahem Begin of Herut contended that "the U.S. and the Soviet Union had demonstrated
by their shipments of arms to Arab states that they don't care if
Israel is destroyed."[27] Begin recommended a military operation by Israel to drive the Egyptians out of the Gaza Strip.
Meir Argon of Mapai believed that, if arms from any source
were not forthcoming, a situation might develop which would
"force Israel into a defensive war." Mr. Israel Barzilai of
Mapam accused Herut of welcoming the arms deal to give
Israel an excellent excuse for starting a preventive war. "The
Soviet bloc," maintained Barzilai, "had the right to defend
itself against American attempts to set up bases in the Middle
East, but this did not give it the right to strengthen aggres-
sors."[28] Esther Wilenska of the Communist party called the
arms deal a commercial agreement for Egyptian self-defense
against imperialistic pressure. Wilenska elaborated by saying
that "Israel too could receive arms from the Soviet bloc if it
would follow Egypt's example, and declare its independence
from military alliances."[29]

On October 31, 1955, Israeli Prime Minister, Moshe
Sharett, met with V. M. Molotov, the Soviet Foreign Minister,
in Geneva. At that time Sharett complained that the arms deal

with Egypt was contrary to the "Geneva Spirit" of settling international disputes by peaceful means.[30] However, the Soviets were evasive each time the arms deal issue was raised. The Western powers also raised the issue with Soviet officials. John Foster Dulles, the U.S. Secretary of State, warned the Soviets that the arms deal would make war a likely possibility in the Middle East.[31] Also, the British expressed their displeasure when Harold Macmillan, the British Foreign Secretary, shared with Molotov his concern that the arms deal might spark an arms race in the Middle East.[32]

Arms Sent to Syria

Ignoring these warnings, the Soviet leaders continued to pursue their offensive in the Middle East. After the arms deal became public on September 27, 1955, the Soviets could support the Arab states openly. On October 2, 1955, the Premiers and Foreign Ministers of Syria, Jordan, and Lebanon met in Damascus to discuss the possibility of buying arms from the Soviet bloc.[33] Negotiating with the Soviet Union became the order of the day. The Syrian Premier met with Serge Nemchin, the Soviet Ambassador in Damascus, to discuss Soviet arms to Syria, but the results were not made public. However, by March, 1956, Czechoslovakian arms began to reach Syria.[34] On October 23, 1955, Moscow Radio broadcast a statement by TASS, the Soviet News Agency, that the Soviet bloc had not offered arms to Israel. TASS was refuting a report by the U.S. State Department that the Soviet bloc was ready to supply arms to Israel as well as to the Arab countries.[35]

Nasser and Khrushchev

In spite of the pro-Egyptian policy of the Soviet Union in 1955, there is evidence to indicate[36] that Khrushchev, after having given arms and other aid to Egypt, never entirely

Art Bimrose, in The Portland Oregonian, *captures the Western view of Nasser as an Arab nationalist leader who is uncritically enticed to plunge into the Soviet waters only to suffer disaster when caught by the Soviet monster lurking unexpectedly below the surface.*

trusted Nasser in terms of the possibility that the latter might return Egypt to the "Western camp." On the other hand, Nasser was always apprehensive about (1) an eventual East-West agreement at the Arabs' expense; (2) the continual pressure from Khrushchev to ease up on the measures against Egyptian Communists; and (3) the Soviet interference in Arab unity. Soviet interference in Arab unity did occur in Iraq after the Kassem coup of 1958.

Subtle reminders of each party's bargaining strengths surfaced from time to time in the bi-lateral diplomacy between

Egypt and the Soviet Union. The latter was uniquely in a
position to radically change the very nature of Israel by dou-
bling that country's population if it should decide to allow
Jews freely to emigrate. Ben Ami relates a humorous anec-
dotal story, told to him by Jews in the Soviet Union, of one
meeting between Khrushchev and Nasser:

> When the Egyptian ruler, Nasser, visited the Soviet Union and
> met Khrushchev, they conducted long and intimate talks. At one
> of the talks the problem of Egyptian communists was raised, for
> Egypt was at that time arresting and jailing communists. The dis-
> cussion became deadlocked; the atmosphere grew heavy and
> strained. Then Khrushchev said to Nasser: "Suppose we let this
> ride for the time being and take up some non-controversial is-
> sues."

> "Go ahead," Nasser replied.
> Khrushchev said: "I'd like to tell you about some data from the
> central statistical bureau of the Soviet Union. It might be of inter-
> est to you."
> "Please do," said Nasser.
> Khrushchev went on: "My statisticians tell me that among the
> three million Jews living in the Soviet Union, there are about a
> half a million of military age, and those include several thousand
> trained flight engineers and pilots, several thousand weapons and
> armored car experts, a few thousand military engineers, several
> thousand military doctors, several hundred rocket experts and
> capable nuclear scientists, several thousand . . ."
> Nasser interrupted and said: "Let's go back to the previous
> subject. I'm willing to promise . . ."[37]

Soviet policy in the Middle East was also affected by
inter-Arab politics. On October 19, 1955, Egypt and Syria concluded a military pact for common defense.[38] A Supreme Defense Command composed of the Premiers and Defense
Ministers of both countries was set up. Arab propaganda emphasized the pact as created to oppose Israel; from the Soviet
point of view, it was a bulwark against the Baghdad Pact. It

served at this time to reassure the Soviet Union that its trust in Egypt as genuinely and permanently opposed to the Western pact was warranted. This was, however, not the first military pact between the two states. On March 3, 1955, a less publicized military agreement had been made under conditions of fewer commitments by each party.[39] Already at this time both Egypt and the Soviet Union viewed it as a counterforce to the Baghdad Pact. Both of the treaties with Syria embodied Nasser's determination to oppose any Western sponsored Middle East alliance against the Soviet Union. It is not inconceivable that Nasser also designed the March 3, 1955, military pact to influence the ongoing Middle East debate in the Kremlin toward favorable considerations of Egypt in the wake of the bloody Israeli retaliatory raid against Egyptian troops in the Gaza Strip, February 28, 1955. The Kremlin decision-makers must have discussed the problems of Egypt's weakness.

By the end of 1955, the Soviet attitude toward the Middle East was clear: an open support of the Arab States, and hostility toward Israel. On December 29, 1955, Khrushchev made a report to the Supreme Soviet on his trip to India, Burma, and Afghanistan. In it he also discussed the Middle East:

> . . . We understand the aspirations of the peoples of the Arab countries who are fighting for complete liberation from foreign dependence. At the same time the actions of Israel, which from the very days of its existence began to threaten its neighbors and to pursue an unfriendly policy toward them, should be condemned. It is clear that this policy does not answer Israel's national interests, that well-known imperialist powers stand behind those who are carrying this policy. They are bent on using Israel as their tool against the Arab peoples, having in mind the exploitation of the natural resources of this region. . . .[40]

NOTES

1. See Michael Brecher, *The Foreign Policy System of Israel* (New Haven: Yale University Press, 1972), p. 253. Brecher discusses the contrasting personality styles of David Ben Gurion and Moshe Sharett as a factor in policy decision-making in Israel.

2. United Nations Security Council, *Official Records, 693rd Meeting,* March 17, 1955, p. 5.

3. Mohammed Hassanein Heikal, *The Cairo Documents* (Garden City, New York: Doubleday & Co., 1973), pp. 46–47.

4. Uri Ra'anan, *The USSR Arms the Third World* (Cambridge, Mass.: The MIT Press, 1969), p. 137.

5. *Al-Ahram,* April 1, 1955, p. 9.

6. Ibid.

7. For a discussion of the Baghdad Pact as a factor in Soviet Middle East policy, see Arthur Jay Klinghoffer, "Context and Pretext: Evaluating the Soviet Role in the Middle East," *Mizan* 10 (May–June 1968): 86–93.

8. *Pravda,* April 17, 1955, p. 1, as cited in the *Current Digest of the Soviet Press,* VII, No. 16, June 1, 1955, pp. 18–19.

9. *Pravda,* April 24, 1955, p. 3, as cited in the *Current Digest of the Soviet Press,* VII, No. 17, June 8, 1955, p. 17.

10. *Al-Ahram,* April 18, 1955, p. 17.

11. Ibid., p. 1.

12. Ibid., p. 13.

13. N. A. Bulganin, "Speech at the Warsaw Conference," *Supplement to New Times,* No. 21 (May, 1955), pp. 7, 9.

14. Heikal, p. 48.

15. Ibid., p. 49.

16. Ibid.

17. U.S., Congress, House, Committee on Foreign Affairs, *Mutual Security Act of 1954,* Hearing, 83rd Cong., 2nd Sess., May 3, 1954 (Washington: Government Printing Office, 1954), p. 473.

18. *Jerusalem Post,* August 4, 1955, p. 1.

19. Ibid., September 30, 1955, p. 1.

20. Avigdor Dagan, *Moscow and Jerusalem* (New York: Abelard-Schuman, 1970), p. 91.

21. *Jerusalem Post,* September 30, 1955, p. 4.

22. Ibid., October 3, 1955, p. 4.

23. Ibid.

24. Ibid.

25. Ibid., October 4, 1955, p. 1.

26. Ibid., October 19, 1955, p. 2.

27. Ibid., p. 1.

28. Ibid.

29. Ibid.

30. Ibid., November 1, 1955, p. 1.

31. Dwight D. Eisenhower, *Waging Peace, 1956*–1961 (Garden City, New York: Doubleday & Company, 1965), p. 25.

32. Dallin, *Soviet Foreign Policy After Stalin* (New York: J. B. Lippincott Co., 1961), p. 395.

33. *Jerusalem Post*, October 3, 1955, p. 1.

34. Dallin, p. 397.

35. *Jerusalem Post*, October 24, 1955, p. 1.

36. See Heikal, *Cairo Documents*, pp. 121–27.

37. Ben Ami, *Between Hammer and Sickle* (Philadelphia: The Jewish Publication Society, 1967), pp. 262–63.

38. *Jerusalem Post*, October 20, 1955, p. 1.

39. *Al-Ahram*, March 4, 1955, p. 1.

40. *Pravda & Izvestia*, December 30, 1955, pp. 3–5, as cited in the *Current Digest of the Soviet Press*, VII, No. 52, February 8, 1956, p. 19.

CHAPTER 10

Pro-Arab, Anti-Israel: Soviet Policy Is Crystallized

The dramatic events of 1956 completed the 180-degree Soviet policy reversal from the 1947 support of Israel against the Arabs, to a pro-Arab policy against Israel. The Soviet policy occurred not by grand design but by reacting to opportunities as they developed in the Middle East. More specifically, Moscow's objective of reducing the Western influence and replacing it with a Soviet presence, or at least a pro-Soviet leaning, was accomplished by cashing in on (1) the Arab sensitivities to Western imperialism on the part of the rising new generation of Arab nationalists and (2) the Arab antagonism to Israel armed and sustained by Western aid. The year 1956 was simply a year of splendid opportunities for the Soviet Union. In retrospect, at least, it was a very simple strategy which could be and would be achieved by an amazingly low-risk policy—just present the Soviet Union on the Arab side in the latter's widespread and bitter feeling against Israel and Western imperialism in the Middle East. The Soviet's unexpected success was helped along by the striking inability of the Western powers to develop a common policy toward Nasser once the issues were drawn over the latter's nationalization of the Suez Canal.[1]

1956: The Year of the Suez Canal

The crucial events of 1956 focused on the Suez Canal zone, i.e., the departure of the last of the British military; the nationalization of the Canal; the Israeli, French, and British military invasion of Sinai and the Canal zone; etc. These events evolved from important political decisions of international politics made in 1955 and earlier. In the Geneva conferences of 1955, significant East-West efforts were made to blunt new and rising perils resulting from the rehabilitation of Germany, but the efforts were unsuccessful.

The reasons for the 1955 conferences were many. By the mid-1950s both sides had mastered the secrets of the hydrogen bomb. It was felt that a summit conference might be able to defuse the threatening international situation. East-West meetings of heads of state had not been held since 1945. Since the fall of 1954 the Soviet Union had been suggesting a summit conference to deal with the high political pressure area of central Europe. Disarmament agreements and central European security treaties were proposed solutions which Moscow wanted to explore with the Western powers. Britain, France, and the United States saw political dangers in the Soviet proposal. It was felt that the Soviets might destroy the fragile unity within NATO over issues such as rearmament, sovereignty, and NATO membership for West Germany. The three major Western allies agreed on a summit meeting with Soviet Russia only after the success in signing the Paris treaties giving sovereignty to the Western occupation zone of Germany, and integrating the new state into NATO defense.

Neither the Geneva summit meeting (July 18–23, 1955) nor the later Geneva foreign ministers' meeting (October 27–November 11, 1955) succeeded in the task of dealing with the nuclear threat and the deterioration of security in central Europe, even though this was originally felt to be, in 1955, an opportune and urgent time for handling this matter. At Geneva, the Soviets pushed for disarmament and a European security treaty *before* western Germany rearmed as a major NATO partner; the United States argued, on the other hand, that agreement on German reunification was a *prior* necessity. (Presumably Secretary of State Dulles also thought in terms of extracting a price for agreeing to the Soviets' need to reduce military expenditures stemming from Moscow's domestic political pressures for consumer goods.)

The failure of Geneva in 1955 served to influence a new Soviet, post-Stalin, foreign policy away from Europe toward the third world states, which had renewed their determination to play a "positive neutralist" role in world politics at the Bandung Conference a few months earlier (April, 1955).

Bulganin and Khrushchev's month-long trip (November 18–December 19, 1955) to India, Burma, and Afghanistan should be seen as a reaction to the Geneva deadlock in Europe and as a new vision of Soviet opportunities after the death of Stalin. This new Khrushchev vision was also exemplified in the Middle East by the Czech arms deal with Egypt, arranged by Moscow and announced in September.

By 1956 *change* was the order of the day—or, as the scholars characterized it, the Middle East had become a politically fluid situation. Eisenhower and Dulles were dismayed at the adverse turn of events for U.S. policy in the previous twelve months. Important events contributing to the political destabilization of the Middle East were: (1) the creation of the Baghdad Pact (February 24, 1955) which was an event of major antagonism to both Cairo and Moscow; (2) the bloody Israeli retaliatory raid against the Egyptian troops in Gaza (February 28, 1955) which humiliated Nasser and added insult to the Western arms embargo against him; (3) the Bandung Conference (April, 1955) which catapulted Nasser to international fame as a third world nationalist; (4) Nasser's breaking of the Western arms embargo (announced September 27, 1955)—an event of serious liabilities for Western interests as seen at the time; and (5) the escalation of Arab organized raids into Israel—particularly from the Egyptian held territory of the Gaza Strip and from Sinai.

The rising Arab–Israeli antagonism, furthermore, added to American difficulties in terms of domestic politics as the pro-Israel lobby increased its pressure on the government to supply arms to Israel to maintain the Middle East's military balance.

Foreign Policy Failures Dumped in UN Lap

There seemed to be no end to Washington's dilemmas. There were strong pressures to join the Baghdad Pact, pressures for and against supplying arms to Israel, and pressures to use both the carrot and the stick in keeping Nasser from any further alignment with the Soviet Union. In the end, the United States took the easy way out; it decided to avoid the hard choices and moralize the dilemma in the United Nations. In the spring of 1956 President Eisenhower called on the United Nations to take "urgent" action to avoid a Middle East arms race. Peace was to be maintained by restraints on both sides in conformity with the UN directives resulting from that body's involvement in the area. More specifically, the United States pushed for a strong initiative by the Secretary General to meet with the conflicting parties and confront them with UN demands for a peace settlement. The United States and Israel would benefit by a maintenance of the status quo—to be accepted by the Arabs in a formal peace treaty. Egypt and other Arab states, however, defined their national interests in terms of maintaining the tension. Their interests lay in changing the status quo. For both international and domestic reasons, heat was to be kept on Israel.

In reference to the Security Council, the Arab delegates pursued a strategy of curbing the UN's peace-making initiatives. They pushed for a resolution which would reduce the Secretary-General's freedom of action, limiting his efforts to that of securing compliance to the armistice agreements. Since the Arab states were not members of the Security Council, they could not vote. Yet the Soviets insisted that the Arabs be allowed to participate in the Council's debate; the Russians refused to participate unless the major Arab states were first allowed to speak in the Security Council.

Opposing the Western position, the Soviet Union became the champion of the Arab states and succeeded in reducing the power of the UN to pressure peace upon the area. The outcome for the West was failure. Efforts to take the easy way out

Palmer, in The Springfield [Mo.] Leader Press, *captures the dismay in the West when the Soviet Union sided with the Arabs and stopped UN Security Council resolutions which were critical of the Arab states.*

'GO ON—I'M BACKING YOU UP, COMRADE'

The rising nationalism of the Arab Middle East pushing to "eat up" (to eliminate) the Western interests in the Middle East was seen by the West as a means of "fattening" the Arab states for the Soviet appetite which would then devour the Middle East. (Haynie in The Greensboro [N. C.] Daily News)

and use the low cost mechanism of the United Nations to deal with the Middle East dilemmas of American foreign policy were basically unsuccessful. Secretary-General Hammarskjold's mission did succeed in reducing, at least temporarily, the border incidents, but the result was far short of

U. S. goals. In a sense the abortive effort of the United States in the UN had opened "Pandora's box" for the expansion of Soviet effectiveness in penetrating the Arab Middle East.

The new Soviet government leadership seized the initiative in utilizing the UN as a means of demanding for itself an expanded influence in the Middle East politics. With a veto in the Security Council, and by supporting the Arab member states, Moscow accumulated the clout necessary to erode the West's post-war claim to the Middle East as its exclusive sphere of influence—a claim pointedly demonstrated by the tripartite agreement of May, 1950.

Historical Events Leading to "the Explosion over Suez" (1956)

In April (1956) Bulganin and Khrushchev made a "goodwill" visit to England. While the British were hosting the two leaders, the Soviet government reaffirmed its demand of playing a role in the international politics of the Middle East.

The crucial 1956 events as related to Egypt involved the termination of the British military presence in Egypt, controversy over the Suez Canal, the international politics of financing the Aswan Dam, and the impact of the 1955 Soviet arms deal upon the Arab-Israeli conflict. In brief historical review, the British military presence in Egypt was legally based upon the Anglo-Egyptian Treaty of 1936 which limited the British military force in Egypt to 10,000 troops and set the conditions under which these were to be exclusively concentrated in the huge British Suez military base.

The Korean War

As already mentioned, it was the outbreak of the Korean War in June, 1950, which created a new Western urgency to

Great Britain found its sprawling military base on the banks of the Suez Canal increasingly unpopular with the rising strength of Egyptian nationalists in the post-World War II era of anti-colonialism. In the 1950s, after the shock of the Korean invasion in Asia, the United States increasingly encouraged Britain to pull out of Suez in the hope that Egypt could be won over as a willing participant in the proposed Middle East defense alliance against the Soviet threat. (Seibel in The Richmond Times-Dispatch)

extend NATO's southern flank via a Middle East defense organization officially designated as the Allied Middle East Command. The greatest hurdle was Egypt, where antagonism to British imperialism set limits to what even the ruling Wafd party could support. To increase the chances of success, the Western powers decided in mid-October, 1951, to invite Egypt, first of all, to participate in the defense organization. Not only was this refused, the Wafd leadership pushed through official government action which unilaterally abrogated (1) the 1899 treaty of joint Anglo–Egyptian sovereignty over the Sudan and (2) the 1936 treaty which provided for the British military presence in Egypt. Britain, of course, refused to accept this unilateral action, and its troops in Egypt were able to insure the "British interpretation of events." Nevertheless, Egyptian opposition and terrorist activities against the Suez base (beginning in 1951) reduced its military value and added to the pressures for Great Britain to leave Egypt.

The Nasser Coup

The Wafd action was, of course, very popular at the time, but it became a political trap for the party when, as time went by, it "couldn't deliver." Along with the monarchy, the government of Egypt became increasingly discredited. It was this situation which provided Nasser and his group of Free Officers the opportunity to destroy the old political order in the successful coup of July 22–23, 1952.

The Free Officers assured the British of the safety of their nationals and were willing to recognize, for the present, the existing British interests. This won them British support, which was important for the success of the coup. As a long term objective of foreign policy, however, the Free Officers were determined to remove the British military presence from Egypt. The Soviets gave this strong, if "low risk," support. Moscow had originally been very critical of the Nasser coup in terms of any benefits the event might have for Soviet interests.

The Sudan Treaty

In any case, the Free Officers, now under the titular head of General Mohammed Naguib, succeeded in working out a solution with the British in relation to the Sudan (October 6, 1953). Nasser and Naguib believed Egypt's position to be strong enough to accept "national self-determination" for the Sudan, for it seemed to them the Sudan would inevitably come to some kind of attachment to Egypt.

The Anglo–Egyptian Treaty of 1954

The Russians, understandably, became increasingly uneasy about Egypt when the 1954 Anglo-Egyptian treaty dealing with the British military base at Suez was announced—an agreement that had to await the outcome of bitter domestic rivalry between Nasser and Naguib.

The 1954 treaty involved considerable concessions on both sides, and the Soviet government was concerned that Nasser had compromised to the extent of settling all outstanding issues with the West and would now lead Egypt into the Western camp. In any case, because of the British re-appraisal of their defensive needs, such as (1) the Egyptian antagonism to the continued British presence which had reduced the military value of the base, (2) the American pressure on the British to trade the base for a "willing Egyptian ally," and (3) the changed natured of military defense due to the successful testing of the hydrogen bomb, Anglo–Egyptian relations were again established on an official treaty basis. The treaty was signed on October 19, and it provided for the phasing out of all British military personnel over the next twenty months. The Suez base facilities would be maintained by no more than 800 British civilian technicians who would hire up to 400 Egyptian nationals to make up the necessary additional labor force to maintain the facility for another seven years. The British military would have the right to reactivate the base in case of an attack "by a foreign power" on any member of the Arab

League or on Turkey (an attack on Israel or Iran was excluded from this right). Egypt, for its part, agreed to respect the 1888 Convention of Constantinople in operating the Suez Canal, and to give the RAF full landing rights and service facilities in the Canal Zone. In spite of the fact that Nasser felt he had driven a good bargain with the British, the Russians were apprehensive about Nasser's compromises and about Egypt now swinging back toward the Western camp in its foreign policy.

Before the last British officer left Egypt on June 13, 1956, Nasser saw opportunities in moving Egypt into a more pro-Soviet policy. He was sensitive to domestic criticism, of being a "Western lackey" whenever he reached agreement with the West in dealing with inevitable conflicts of interest. After all, he had built an important base of political support on anti-Western colonialism and thus could not afford to allow all outstanding differences to be settled. He seemingly hesitated to accept Western offers for financing the Aswan High Dam without compensating gestures toward the Eastern bloc. If he suspended anti-Baghdad Pact propaganda—which he did for a

Progress ...

A British view emphasizing the irony of Middle East nationalists escaping through the door of British colonialism only to be enticed by the Soviet Union—by the offer of food, money, and arms—to innocently walk into an even more harsh colonial prison. (Cummings in the London Daily *Express)*

Guess We've Got Company

MINNEAPOLIS TRIBUNE

By mid-1956 the Dulles foreign policy had backfired; Egypt and the Soviet Union had established close relations and the West (the United States) became "the odd man out." (Reprinted with permission from the Minneapolis Tribune)

while—as a compromise gesture, his domestic critics could charge him with a sell-out to Western imperialism.

Britain and the United States viewed with disfavor the burgeoning Soviet impact upon Egypt. The Soviet arms shipments to Egypt and Syria tended to exceed even the earlier fears. Trade agreements, technical missions, and various other varieties of exchanges added to the West's apprehensions about the goals Nasser had for Egypt, and raised questions about the long term advisability of dealing with Nasser in terms of trying to promote friendly relations with Egypt through various concessions and promises.

The Pro-Soviet Bias in June 18 Celebrations

High level Soviet representatives were received for the June 18 celebrations officially ending the British occupation of the Canal Zone. The Egyptian national holiday seemed to have been deliberately rigged to carry a pro-Soviet, anti-Western flavor. Nasser emphasized Egypt's "positive neutralist" foreign policy, which disappointed American hopes for Egypt's basic Western orientation after the Suez military base had been relinquished and offers made to finance the Aswan Dam. The new Soviet foreign minister, Dmitri Shepilov, was sent to Egypt to participate with "high visibility" in the June 18 to 23 festivities marking the end of British colonialism in Egypt. President Nasser, in the Evacuation Day celebrations at Port Said (June 18), raised the Egyptian flag and addressed the audience in terms of Egypt's " 'rendezvous with destiny when it saw the remnants of the foreign invader sneak out, back to where they came from.' "[2]

On display in the Alexandria harbor on June 18 were two destroyers delivered to Egypt by the Soviets only seven days before the Evacuation Day festivities.

Aswan Dam Politics

As the representative of the Soviet Union, Foreign Minister Shepilov took the occasion to ostensibly increase the

Soviet offer of aid for the Aswan High Dam. According to Egyptian sources, the USSR increased its offer for building the dam to £ 500 million involving a twenty-year loan at 2% interest.[3] After the shock of the Czech arms deal, Washington had rushed George Allen to Cairo to seek not only a nullification of Egypt's arms tie with the Soviet Union, but also to indicate a renewed urgency in the Western financing of the dam. This was the project which an ambitious, if not vain, Nasser wished to leave as his legacy to Egypt—a monument which might well overshadow Pharoah Cheop's timeless memorial and the other great pyramids of Ancient Egypt.

On October 17 the Egyptian Ambassador in Washington, Ahmed Hussein, had a detailed discussion with Dulles concerning the financing of the dam. Ambassador Hussein told the U. S. Secretary of State that " 'it was essential Egypt should have the support of the United States in building the High Dam.' " Hussein continued his version of the meeting by saying, " 'I told him that despite the fact that the Russian government had offered us better conditions than those offered by the World Bank to finance the project, we still preferred to deal with the World Bank.' "[4] This statement by Hussein is contradicted by Mohammed Hassanein Heikal, Nasser's confidant and an Egyptian journalist of world stature, who maintained Ambassador Hussein's statement to Dulles was a bluff; the Russians had never actually made such an offer.[5]

On December 17, 1955, Washington had offered the financial package to Egypt. It involved financing the first stage of the dam with $56 million from the United States, $14 million from Great Britain, and $200 million from the World Bank. There were certain conditions: Egypt was not to accept any Soviet offer to participate, and agreement was to be obtained from the Sudan concerning the allocation of Nile water and the acceptance of an inundation of the border areas of the Sudanese Nile valley, since the newly formed lake would extend into the Sudan. Furthermore, some pledges of responsibility for the sound management of the Egyptian economy

IMPOSTER IN THE HAREM

After the Soviet arranged arms shipments to Egypt, this political cartoonist captured the West's apprehension about the Middle East in the following depiction. (Reprinted with permission from the Minneapolis Tribune)

were requested by the World Bank—a very sensitive issue for the Cairo regime which had only recently escaped from the impact of British influence along these lines.

NEW SCENERY

Important Middle East developments in 1956 included the recognition of Red China by Egypt. The rise of the Peoples' Republic of China was still a very emotional issue in the United States, and Nasser's developing affinity with Peking made the Congress (whose action was required for funding the proposed Aswan High Dam) "see red." (Reprinted with permission from the Minneapolis Tribune)

Mohammed Hassanein Heikal, writing from the Cairo perspective, insisted that the United States had made two more requirements of Cairo: (1) that "Egypt would make a declaration saying that there would be no more arms deals with the Soviet Union" and (2) that Nasser was "to exercise his leadership in the Middle East and conclude peace between the Arabs and the Israelis."[6]

In any case, what seemed like Egyptian vacillation between East and West to play one side off against the other—in this case to presumably get better terms from the West—was not popular, to say the least, with the American Secretary of State. John Foster Dulles, in addition to his own views of what the national interests of the United States required, was never far removed from looking at international politics through moralizing lenses.

When Khrushchev and Bulganin had suggested in London (April, 1956) that the Soviet Union would be willing to join the West in a United Nations-sponsored Middle East arms embargo (perhaps only a tactical ploy), Nasser became apprehensive enough about such a possibility that he found it advisable to emphasize the "Peking option." This involved establishing diplomatic relations (May 16, 1956) with the People's Republic of China, with the prior requirement that Egypt had to break relations with Chiang's Nationalist China. This event, perhaps more than any other Egyptian action at the time, was criticized in Washington—the Communist regime in China was still a very emotional issue in the United States.

Negotiations for American funding of the Aswan Dam became increasingly drawn out. Egypt's "positive neutralist" policy and, indeed, its occasional public support of the Soviet Union and mainland China created rising antagonism in Washington. President Eisenhower, who was recovering from the ileitis attack, gave Dulles virtually a free hand in the Aswan Dam policy. Heikal's image of the Washington political scene at this time is noteworthy:

> President Eisenhower was convalescing, playing golf after an attack of ileitis, and so Dulles telephoned him and said that the

Egyptians "were not playing ball" and that he proposed to withdraw the High Dam offer. And Eisenhower reportedly said: "Whatever you think, Foster, whatever you think." That was on July 18.[7]

After further negotiation but no agreement, Nasser began to suspect that Dulles was no longer sincere in his desire to reach a funding agreement. Consequently, according to Heikal, Nasser instructed Ahmed Hussein, Egypt's Washington Ambassador, to test the sincerity of the Washington offer by accepting all the American conditions. Hussein arrived back in the United States on July 17; his fateful meeting with Dulles in the Secretary of State's office occurred two days later. With Hussein and Dulles at the meeting were George V. Allen and Undersecretary of State Herbert Hoover, Jr. As related by Allen to Kenneth Love, the encounter of traumatic Middle East impact evolved as follows:

"... Hussein began by saying he was greatly concerned by the Russian offers and the expectations they raised. He eulogized the High Dam, emphasized Nasser's strength of vision, and said how much he, Hussein, wanted the U.S. to do it. He showed that he realized we had problems. But he touched his pocket and said 'We've got the Soviet offer right in our pocket.' This gave Dulles his cue. Eisenhower had said often that the first person to say such a thing, he'd tell him to go to Moscow.

Dulles didn't read the statement which was released to the press immediately afterward but more or less paraphrased it. Dulles' reply was kindly in tone. He said we had seriously considered it and realized how important it was. But frankly, he said, the economic situation makes it not feasible for the US to take part. We have to withdraw our offer."[8]

Nasser Shocked by Dam Cancellation

Dulles' abrupt cancellation of the offer was taken as a personal affront by Nasser; it produced a fateful response which finally ended in war. Nasser received the news while flying back to Egypt from a meeting with Tito in Brioni—a meeting at which Prime Minister Nehru of India had also been present. Heikal describes Nasser's angry reaction in the presence of himself and the venerable Foreign Minister Dr. Mahmoud Fawzi. "'This is not withdrawal.'" "'It is an attack on the [Nasser] regime and an invitation to the people of Egypt to bring it down.'"[9]

To some degree Dulles felt vindicated when two days later Shepilov acknowledged in Moscow that there was no specific Soviet offer to build the dam—the lack of a Soviet offer was rationalized as a result of the fact that Egypt had never made a request for financing the dam.

Domestic opposition in the United States to the funding of the dam came, in varying degrees, from a number of sources. There was the pro-Israel lobby with well-established roots on the Washington scene. This group insisted on bargaining with Egypt for Israeli rights to use the Suez Canal. In addition, the South's cotton lobby attacked the proposal in terms of opposing the Aswan Dam's expansion of cotton production in Egypt, because there was already a world cotton glut. No taxpayer's money should be spent for increasing the world cotton supplies when tax money was already being used to subsidize American cotton farmers. Finally, the China lobby, through spokesmen such as Senators William Knowland and Walter Judd, sharply criticized Egypt for recognizing Communist China—particularly because it required the breaking of diplomatic relations with Nationalist China. In addition, 1956 was an election year; Congress was very sensitive to Nasser's generally bad image in the American press and with the general public. Some senators approached Dulles with express reservations about U.S. aid for this Egyptian project. In the end, the Senate Appropriations Committee approved a foreign aid appropriation bill which specifically *excluded* the use of any monies for the Aswan High Dam without another act of Congress. Various groups with concerns for national security insisted it was unwise to send more aid to neutralist states than to states which had faithfully supported the West in the cold war with the Soviet Union.

Egypt Nationalizes the Canal

The abrupt cancellation had its repercussions also in the domestic politics of Egypt. Nasser felt humiliated and offended. His "righteous indignation" was effectively shared with the Egyptian public. Dulles' action was primarily responsible for Nasser's decision on July 26, 1956, to nationalize the Suez Canal company—exactly a week after the fateful Washington meeting with Hussein. A very dangerous chain of events had now been set in motion.

British and French Reaction

The nationalization was the "straw" which Britain and France now felt compelled to use to break "the Egyptian camel's back." It was "the last straw" of French and British patience with Nasser. Nasser would have to go. He was compared to Hitler in systematically destroying their interests in the Middle East, and they insisted this ultimately unacceptable destruction would continue until stopped by force.

We shall not relate here the fascinating, if tragic, sequence of events triggered by the nationalization, i.e., the "Greek tragedy" as it was played out in the domestic politics of Britain; the almost inconceivable initiatives and responses—or lack of them—among the major NATO allies; the otherwise incongruent alignment of Britain, France, and Israel in secret collusion, joining forces for war against Egypt; the simultaneous uprisings in Poland and—particularly—Hungary against Moscow's own brand of colonialism over them; etc. It would be interesting to trace the drama of political events as they unfolded, but we must restrict ourselves to the primary focus

"The other's troubles are funnier."

Alexander, in The Philadelphia Bulletin, *depicts the delight each side found in observing the other side's embarrassment resulting from the nationalism of peoples under its domination.*

of the impact these events had on Soviet relations with Israel and the Arabs.

By the second half of 1956 there had developed, perhaps by coincidence rather than by design, a common antagonism in Western states against Egypt. France's major quarrel with Nasser stemmed not from the Baghdad Pact, but from the moral support and tangible aid the latter was giving to the Algerian rebels in the bitter conflict taking place there. Largely through the initiative of the military, France was engineering shipments of modern military supplies to Israel as a threat, or for actual use, against Egypt. Britain was particularly incensed by Nasser's power in Iraq and Jordan, in using his appeal to the masses as "street power" against their own pro-British governments there. Threats to important British interests were at stake and it became very popular in Britain to think of "cutting Nasser down to size." Especially galling was the incident of Jordan's abrupt dismissal of John Glubb, early in 1956, from his commanding role in the Jordanian military forces. In the British view, it was also Nasser who was significantly responsible for Lebanon and Syria (as well as Jordan) turning down invitations to join the Baghdad Pact.

The United States was also unhappy about Nasser's influence over the Arab masses in these states, but the greatest antagonism stemmed from, as already mentioned, the May, 1956, action to establish official relations with Peking, and from the new relationship with Moscow.

Israel Apprehensive of Nasser

At this time Israel was also feeling an increased threat to national security. The Anglo–Egyptian treaty of October, 1954, (providing for removal of British troops from the Suez base within twenty months) eliminated, in the Israeli view, a restraining factor to Egypt's unstable and unpredictable military dictatorship. Nasser might be pressured by nationalists of the left or the right into a military action to keep the regime in power. Indeed this seemed to have happened after the Gaza raid of February 28, 1955. Nasser unleashed the fedayeen for raids into Israel during March, April, and May, and then again after August 22. Nasser decided to resort to the same tactics used with some success earlier against the superior British military forces at the Suez base—a hit and run, guerrilla harrassment which contributed to getting the British out.

Nasser, for political reasons both domestic and pan-Arab, could not afford to make peace with Israel. As long as Israel and a Western presence remained, Nasser could not afford to eliminate his anti-Israel and anti-Western positions since it was upon these nationalistic issues that he had built his base of political support—his hero image as a "modern-day Saladin."

Israel refused to accept the permanent prohibition of its ships from the Strait of Tiran and the Suez Canal. Nasser could not afford the adverse impact on his political aspirations if he changed policy and allowed Israeli ships through these two waterways. Cairo refused to accept the 1951 United Nations Security Council resolution which requested Egypt to allow Israel to use the canal. Nasser rationalized the refusal on the grounds that Egypt and Israel were still at war.

The impending Anglo-Egyptian treaty (actually signed later on October 19, 1954) provided an opportunity for Israel to push for its right to use the canal. Israel felt it might be possible to convince the British to hold out for this Egyptian concession to Israel before approving the treaty. After all, the Egyptians were very anxious to get the British troops out, as provided for in the agreement. Israel decided to act by sending one of its merchant ships, the *Bat Galim*, to Suez on September 28, 1954, to test its right to use the canal. The ship was seized and the crew jailed. The Lavon Affair, discussed previously, should also be seen in the context of the forboding chain of events. Other incidents such as the continuous threat to Israeli lives and property by frequent Arab infiltrators into Israel provided additional reasons for ultimately resorting to a military solution. With the return of Ben Gurion to lead the Jerusalem government in July, 1955, Israel became predisposed to the use of force in dealing with what it considered to be threats from the Arab world.

Israel had earlier felt an increased threat to its security in the period of 1953 to 1955 when both the British and the United States moved in pro-Arab directions at Israel's expense. The British, beginning with the 1953 agreement with Egypt concerning the Sudan and continuing into the post 1954 Suez base settlement, veered toward a pro-Arab position, much to the apprehensions of Jerusalem. In a public speech in London on November 9, 1955,[10] Prime Minister Anthony Eden suggested a territorial settlement between Israel and the Arabs which would involve an Israeli concession of territory to a line somewhere between the prevailing de facto boundaries and the original ones proposed by the UN in 1947. Once the concession was agreed upon, Britain would be willing to guarantee it.

Israel also became apprehensive about U.S. policy. The

new Republican administration, which took office in January, 1953, tended to move toward a more pro-Arab position— again, much to the concern of Israel. Secretary of State Dulles returned from his "maiden trip" to the Middle East in the summer of 1953 with the proclamation that the United States should be more impartial in its Middle East policy. Said Dulles, ". . . the United States should seek to allay the deep resentment against it that has resulted from the creation of Israel." He went on to say we must recognize the Arab fears "that the United States will back the new State of Israel in aggressive expansion."[11]

In October, 1953, President Eisenhower sent Eric Johnston as his personal representative to work out a plan for the allocation of Jordan River water among the riparian states. In the meantime, Israel began the implementation of her own unilaterally adopted plan for the utilization of the Jordan waters, ignoring Washington's request to halt. Dulles then stepped in to stop the Israeli operation on October 20, 1953, by cutting off economic aid to Israel. Aid was restored when Israel agreed to abandon the project.

The United States also supported United Nations censures of Israeli retaliatory strikes into the Arab border states. In a speech on May 1, 1954, Assistant Secretary of State Henry Byroade even went as far as to recommend that Israel restrict immigration in order to reduce the Arab felt threat of future expansion. Israel became alarmed at U.S. policy to the point of making a formal protest to Washington. On August 26, 1955, Secretary of State Dulles made an American proposal for the settlement of the Arab-Israeli dispute. In a vein similar to the British proposal, it included provisions for Israeli territorial concessions to the Arabs, but it also included plans for the return of as many of the 900,000 Palestinian refugees "as may be feasible."[12]

The United States started to back away from these constraints against Israel after the Egyptian arms deal with the Soviets was announced September 27, 1955, then moved still farther away from the previous pro-Egyptian thrusts in the

1956 events of (1) Egypt's recognition of Peking and (2) the nationalization of the canal. By spring of 1956, Great Britain's relations with Cairo had also cooled—particularly over Nasser's opposition to the Baghdad Pact and his role in destroying Britain's position in Jordan in early 1956. By mid-October, 1956, Britain was willing to collude with Israel in overthrowing Nasser.

France's Middle East policy added another dimension to the events. As mentioned, in 1952–53 French foreign policy began veering toward Israel. When Cairo became more supportive of Algerian nationalists in the bitter hostilities there, France moved to align itself more decisively with Israel in 1955 and 1956. To an important degree it was the French initiative, after Egypt's nationalization of the canal, and the French guarantee of support which satisfied Prime Minister Ben Gurion and figured in Israel's decision to lead the tripartite military action against Egypt in the fall of 1956.[13]

A British view of the 1956 Suez Crisis. Prime Minister Anthony Eden is being badly burned while the American Secretary of State John Foster Dulles pretends to be unaware of a crisis. (Cummings in the London Daily Express)

The Tripartite Invasion of Egypt

The Israeli's sweep into Sinai at the end of October, and the British and French invasion in early November, caused considerable ambivalence and anger in Washington—Dulles was caught in embarrassing ignorance of what the United States' own NATO partners (and Israel) were up to. But most importantly, the situation consummated the pro-Arab, anti-Israel trend of Soviet policy in the Middle East.

The de-stabilizing action unfolded as follows. In mid-October, 1956, Britain, France, and Israel reached agreement on a common plan to use military force against Egypt. Politically, if it could be made internationally credible, it was an ingenious and daring plan. Success depended upon secrecy—secrecy not only with regard to timing of the joint invasion, but absolute secrecy of the collusion itself, both before and after the attack. The policy of these three states differed from that of the United States in that the latter opposed the use of military force against Egypt, although it was not opposed to ambiguous public statements hinting at force in order to make Egypt more susceptible to political compromise.

Israel attacked Egypt on the Sinai front in such a manner as to give the impression of only another retaliatory raid in depth. Yet on October 29 a paratroop contingent was dropped behind the Egyptian lines at the eastern approaches to the Mitla Pass only about 40 miles east of the Suez Canal. This strike was an essential part of the tripartite collusion, for the pretext of the French and British invasion was to maintain the operation of the canal in the face of Egyptian-Israeli combat.

Britain and France, according to plan, sent an ultimatum to both Israel and Egypt demanding that each withdraw its forces ten miles from the Suez Canal. This was officially proclaimed as necessary in order to maintain international freedom of passage through the waterway as called for in the 1888 Convention of Constantinople, which Egypt had re-affirmed in the 1954 treaty.

'WHAT'S OUR MIDDLE EAST POLICY TODAY?'

Lewis in The Milwaukee Journal

Lewis, in The Milwaukee Journal, *caricatures vacillations in American Middle East policy by the figures of an anthropomorphized State Department and Uncle Sam sitting on a weather vane.*

'I'll Be Glad To Restore Peace
To The Middle East, Too'

----from <u>Herblock's Special For Today</u> (Simon & Schster, 1958)

*The Herblock cartoon above catches the irony of Soviet "morality"
in offering to help stop the "Western imperialism" of the tripartite
invasion of Egypt (1956) when the USSR just finished a bloody
crushing of the government set up by (what the West called) the
"Hungarian freedom fighters" in Budapest.*

U.S. Policy Shock: From Drift and Ignorance to Anger and Moralism

After the Israeli attack on the 29th, the United States took the initiative in a United Nations Security Council meeting October 30 to restrain Israel. The secret plan, unknown to Britain and France's major NATO ally, the United States, was now put into operation by Britain and France in moving to delay the Israeli censure and by announcing their twelve-hour ultimatum to Israel and Egypt. Although Moscow was on the defensive from UN pressures in the matter of the Hungarian revolution, in which the Hungarian nationalists had risen up in revolt against subservience to the USSR, the latter's tanks moved in to crush the newly independent Budapest government on November 4. With its own international embarrassment eliminated, the Soviet Union was now in a favorable position to gain tremendous political assets in the Arab Middle East by decisively siding with the Arabs in the windfall situation of a serious split among the major NATO allies.

The War

British and French air power was unleashed against selected Egyptian military targets on October 31. Israeli forces captured the Sinai, and Anglo-French paratroops made their assault at Port Said and Port Fuad on November 5 with the seaborne troops coming ashore the following day. With the United States turning against its own allies, the Soviets took the low risk, openly pro-Arab position of publicly threatening to attack Paris and London with nuclear missiles and to send "volunteers" to Egypt to fight the invaders. Moscow's public condemnation of "Israeli aggression" and "renewed Western imperialism" was gratefully received by the Arab world.

.

The Soviets Crush "Freedom Fighters" in Hungary and Protest War in Sinai

At the very time the Soviet Union sent its military forces to crush the successful Hungarian revolution and the new government of Imre Nagy, the Soviet government organized

"Trying to fix it."

NATO is seen as a dismantled clock after the tripartite invasion of Egypt (1956) in which the United States sided with the Soviet Union against Britain and France, its own NATO partners. Roche, in The Buffalo Courier-Express, *captures the dilemma by depicting Uncle Sam as trying to put the NATO clock back together again.*

EUROPEAN VIEWS ON SOVIET POLICY

**"The first batch of volunteer fighters for freedom--
straight from Hungary."**

*The Soviet Union threatened to send volunteers to fight with the
Egyptians against the invading armies of Britain, France, and Israel.
The cartoon above expresses a popular London view of the threat,
which is pictured as a Soviet Trojan Horse containing the same
Soviet troops which had, in a blood bath only a few days earlier,
crushed the Hungarian freedom fighters who had succeeded in
throwing off the Soviet puppet regime in Budapest. (From Associated Newspaper Group Limited, London)*

large-scale, anti-Israeli demonstrations in front of Israel's embassy in Moscow. Any anti-Israel symbolic gestures pleased
the Arabs.

On November 6, 1956, Prime Minister Ben Gurion re-
ceived a sharp note from Bulganin in Moscow characterizing
Israel as "an instrument in the hands of extremist imperialist
Powers" and concluding that Israel's "actions are putting a

question mark on the very existence of Israel as a state."[14] Copies of the message were given to journalists even before it was received by Israel—an indication of the pro-Arab propaganda purpose of the act. In addition, the Soviet Union recalled its ambassador from Israel the same day. The high visibility of its action left little doubt as to Soviet objectives in impressing the Arab world with its anti-Israel, anti-Western position.

Ben Gurion replied to Bulganin's note two days later. Then the Israeli charge d'affaires was handed another note from Bulganin to Ben Gurion on November 15 which continued the criticism. Israel was again criticized as contradicting its professed peaceful intent by being an aggressor state and in collusion with Western imperialism. Israel's attempt to delay withdrawal until its rights to the use of the Suez Canal were secured was considered by Bulganin as unacceptable—an interference in Egypt's sovereignty over the canal. Finally, Bulganin said Israel, France, and Britain were obligated to compensate Egypt for war damages because of their unprovoked aggression.

In the United Nations Shepilov and Kieselev, as spokesmen for the Soviet Union, repeated the anti-Israel position in the public debate. The Soviet delegation, said D. T. Shepilov, considers Israel to have participated in international aggression; it "has played a particularly unedifying, and I might even say provocative, role in the sinister political game of the imperialist forces. . . ."[15]

Kieselev, the Byelorussian delegate, later referred to Israel in a similar way.

As regards Israel, the policy of its extremist groups intent on fanning hostility towards the Arabs and crushing them in reality endangers the cause of peace and is fatal to Israel itself. It is a policy which is solely in the interest of reactionary groups in the United Kingdom and France, anxious to restore colonialism . . . ."[16]

Moscow's Condemnation of Israel and Support for the Arabs

Toward the end of November, *Izvestia* carried a critical commentary on Israel. The Soviet description of the Jewish state's first decade of existence certainly reflected Moscow's new anti-Israel policy; it was now characterized as an aggressive-imperialist nation. Said *Izvestia*:

> By challenging Arab peoples and all peoples struggling against colonialism, Israel is digging its own grave. When in 1947 the United Nations General Assembly decided to establish the State of Israel, the world expected and hoped that Israel would develop on the principles of democracy and peace and would work for peaceful coexistence with its neighbors. These hopes and expectations were not fulfilled. From the very first days of its appearance on the international stage, the State of Israel began threatening its neighbors, following an unfriendly policy toward them, and "Socialists" of the Ben Gurion type put into motion slogans of extremist and aggressive Zionism, placing themselves fully at the disposal of imperialist forces and serving them in all possible ways. The rulers of Israel became the gendarmes of the colonial powers in the Arab East. . . .[17]

The image of Israel in Soviet policy was now essentially synonymous with that of the "imperialist" West seeking to expand its influence and control over the Arabs. The Soviet Union was the new protector of the Arab Middle East. As the *Izvestia* article exemplified, the way to gain favor with the Arabs was to "hate Israel." Even the conservative Arab state of Jordan was not unresponsive to anti-Israeli action. As early as April, 1954, when the Soviet Union took an anti-Israeli stand in the UN Security Council following Israel's retaliatory raid against the Jordanian village of Nahalin (March 28, 1954), the Jordanian parliament officially voted a resolution of appreciation to the USSR.[18] Jordan didn't even have diplomatic relations with the Soviet Union at the time.[19]

It would be inadequate to explain the Soviet Union's pro-Arab policy by only noting Moscow's initiatives. At times Arab states such as Egypt, for its own interests, actively sought this support. Particularly after the 1956 invasion, President Nasser defined Egypt's needs in ways which contributed to the development of closer relations with the Soviet Union. In a general way, Nasser's leadership was confronted with urgent needs both domestic and foreign. For purposes of domestic political stability, the military had to be kept reasonably satisfied. This meant that the arms lost in the Sinai must be replaced. The war had also created grave difficulties for the economy. Western powers, including the United States, froze Egyptian assets in their possession—a situation which created serious hard currency problems for necessary Egyptian imports. Nasser lost the war, but succeeded in reversing the defeat in the post-war international settlement. This success catapulted him to fame in the Arab world. Yet to maintain the hero's role, Nasser had to maintain victories over the enemies of Pan-Arabism—at least propaganda victories. He had to maintain activism in Arab causes. Part of this continuing activism could be seen in his opposition to the Eisenhower Doctrine.

Although not without some contradictions, the Soviet Union was in a position to fulfill Egyptian needs under conditions which furthered the respective national interests of each state. This was not available to the United States with its Israel lobby in domestic politics, its necessary concern for the NATO alliance (a concern which necessitated the rebuilding of positive relations with Britain and France after the 1956 disaster), and its objective of maintaining some kind of a Soviet containment organization on NATO's southern flank. Note that the Baghdad Pact had already been a significant event in bringing the USSR and Egypt together because it was seen in both Moscow and Cairo, each in its own way, as a threat to their security interests.

After the 1956 war, the Soviet Union began replacing the arms captured by Israel or destroyed in the fighting. Egypt,

By 1956 the Soviet Union had mastered the art of riding the magic carpet into the Middle East. While USSR policy was riding high, Western efforts in the Middle East couldn't get off the ground—the old policies seemed frayed and could no longer produce results. (John Stampone in the Army Times*)*

however, was hard pressed for other hard currency imports. The U.S. felt itself in a potentially increased bargaining position vis-à-vis Egypt under these circumstances. Yet in the end, it was the Soviet Union and its satellite states which responded to Nasser's initiatives and supplied the badly needed food, petroleum, fertilizers, and other nonmilitary hard currency imports. These Soviet actions served as additional catalysts to closer Soviet-Egyptian relations.

Nasser and Arab Unity

Nasser gave a high priority to his aspiring position in promoting the cause of Arab unity. He was determined to fulfill the role of the Arabs' leader. As he phrased it in his earlier work, *Egypt's Liberation*, his fulfillment was to be that "role, wandering aimlessly in search of a hero."[20] Nasser could not, or at least would not, sacrifice leadership of the new generation of Arab nationalists, who felt Arab salvation could only come by sweeping away the traditional civilization which was out of tune with the modern world. Arab nationalism condemned the localism of vested interests at the various Arab capitals which fragmented the Arab world and made possible Western imperialism playing off national leaders against each other.

The new generation of Arab nationalists, whom Nasser was determined to lead, (1) supported "revolution from above" in terms of government forcing change—a particular change which they labeled *Arab socialism*; (2) emphasized pan-Arabism in the sense of Arab-wide unity; (3) championed anti-colonialism—removing the unequal treaties and the Western military presence from the Arab Middle East, and (4) advocated modernization, which was necessary in order to be treated as an equal in international politics. Although the official Communist doctrine of atheism was not acceptable to the Islamic roots of Arab civilization, Soviet socialism in the sense of centrally directed economy, state ownership of the means of production, and the use of government power to implement new programs had considerable appeal. In addition, there was no historical experience of Soviet colonialism in Arab lands.

Thus, among the new Arab nationalists the ideology of pan-Arabism with its concept of *socialism* was favorably received. This was exemplified in political organizations such as the Baath Party and, later, the Arab Socialist Union of Egypt.

To remain the effective leader of pan-Arabism, Nasser had to maintain an image of military strength, of being anti-Israel, and of being an Arab leader who could and would stand up to the West—the anti-colonial image. The Soviets were aware of this situation and played their part well. By the end of 1956 Nasser could impress the Arab nationalist movement with his successes; his turning to the Soviets had paid off. He had broken the Western arms embargo by daring to negotiate extensive military supplies from the Soviet Union; he had largely forced the British out of Jordan; he had even eliminated the "mothballed" British Suez base six years prior to the treaty deadline. Moving very effectively from his Arab, third world, and Soviet base of support, Nasser saw the United States come to his aid in compelling the French, British, and Israeli military forces to withdraw entirely from Egyptian territory. The friendship with the Soviet Union had yielded a high payoff for his ambition in leading the new nationalism of the Arab world. Egypt had, for the purposes of its own national interests, made its contribution in bringing the Soviet Union's pro-Arab policy into being.

NOTES

1. See John C. Campbell's discussion, Chapter 8, in *Defense of the Middle East* (New York: Harper & Brothers, 1958).

2. *Facts on File Yearbook 1956*, p. 197.

3. Ibid.

4. Mohammed Hassanein Heikal, *The Cairo Documents* (Garden City, New York: Doubleday & Co., 1973), pp. 58–59.

5. Ibid., p. 59.

6. Ibid., pp. 62–63.

7. Ibid., p. 66. No notation made as to his source of information.

8. Kenneth Love, *Suez the Twice-Fought War* (New York: McGraw-Hill, 1969), p. 315.

9. Heikal, p. 68.

10. *New York Times*, November 10, 1955, p. 1.

11. Harry N. Howard, *The Development of United States Policy in the Near East, South Asia, and Africa During 1953* (Department of State Publication 5432, April 1954).

12. *New York Times*, August 27, 1955, p. 1.

13. Michael Brecher, *Decisions in Israel's Foreign Policy* (London: Oxford University Press, 1974), p. 228.

14. D. T. Shepilov, *Suetskii Vopros (The Suez Question)* (Moscow, 1956), pp. 155–56.

15. United Nations General Assembly, *Official Records, Plenary Meetings*, 11th Session, 592nd Plenary Meeting, Thursday, 23 November 1956.

16. Ibid., 597th Plenary Meeting Tuesday, 27 November 1956.

17. *Izvestia*, November 29, 1956, p. 4.

18. To some degree this action should be considered in light of the radical versus conservative struggle in Jordanian domestic politics at the time, when the more pro-Soviet Fawzi al Mulki temporarily headed the Jordanian cabinet.

19. Diplomatic relations between Jordan and the USSR were not established until 1963.

20. Gamal Abdul Nasser, *Egypt's Liberation* (Washington, D.C.: Public Affairs Press, 1955), p. 87.

Summary

By 1944, eventual victory against Germany had become highly probable. The Soviet Union began to plan for its claim to great power status in post-war international affairs. Except for the border states of Iran and Turkey, the Middle East would receive a secondary, low risk consideration.

To the Soviet Union, the Arab Middle East was not a promising area for spectacular results in foreign policy. The war ended with the Arab world essentially in the British sphere of interest and with a military presence effectively located to control air, land, and sea routes in that strategic area of international politics, as well as to guard the lifeline of oil to the West.

In this situation the Soviet Union decided to use its limited political influence in a manner designed to pry the British out of the Middle East. Communist parties in these basically Muslim lands seemed to be hopelessly weak. National liberation movements were equally hopeless when the war ended. In Soviet eyes, native politicians appeared all too often to have committed themselves to an "understanding" with "imperialist" Britain against the interests of the Arab masses.

Realistically, Moscow saw in the socialist orientation of the Palestine Jews a client group to be backed by the Soviet Union since these Jews had refused to accept the 1939 British White Paper, and were willing to use terror to gain their independence from the British. The acts of sympathy and ideological affinity for this mutuality were carefully nurtured by the Jews during the war.

While the Arabs tended toward a pro-fascist position in World War II, the Jews wholeheartedly joined in the war

against the Axis. Even though already living in conditions of
perilous scarcity, they sacrificed further by giving financial aid
to the war-pressed Russians. For the Jews, these efforts fit into
their plans for a proposed independent state in Palestine after
the wartime catastrophe resulting from, on the one hand,
Germany's extermination camps and from, on the other hand,
the British White Paper of 1939.

In any case, as far as the Soviets were concerned, not only
would it be advisable to reduce the British presence and
exploit Anglo–American differences which developed over
Palestine, it would also be desirable to Balkanize the area and
thereby increase chaos and the chances of acquiring a client
state in the Levant from which to magnify Soviet leverage.
Later, after the creation of Israel, the Soviets sought political
leverage in that country's domestic politics through its
ideological affinity with the Mapam party of Israel (since the
Israeli Communist party was hopelessly weak).

The Soviet Union also felt that by supporting the creation
of a Jewish state in Palestine, it could utilize the link between
the Jews and liberal intellectuals in the United States, and the
Zionists of Palestine to produce a reservoir of pro-Soviet
goodwill in the U.S. Whether in fact this did happen, or to
what degree this was true, still awaits convincing analysis.

As the violence escalated in Palestine and the British
turned the matter over to the United Nations, it was increasingly evident that the Security Council would become involved in terms of its Charter-given responsibility to "maintain international peace and security." As one of the five permanent members of that organ, the Soviet Union saw the possibility of getting Soviet military personnel into Palestine—a
situation which would greatly facilitate the pursuit of its interests there.

Finally, Soviet policy in support of the Jews at the expense
of the Arabs was also a function of the Stalin era of Soviet
domestic politics. As long as Stalin perceived a dichotomous
world of the capitalist-imperialist camp versus the socialist

camp (effectively subservient to Moscow), the possibility of Soviet support of independent liberation movements in the third world was limited. During Stalin's time, the possibilities for Soviet national interests in the Middle East were not effectively explored. The Soviet possibilities for influence in the Arab areas were sharply limited by its 1947 decision to support the creation of a Jewish state in Palestine, which alienated the non-Jewish Middle East.

Soviet foreign policy following World War II concentrated on two consecutive objectives. From 1945 to approximately 1954, Soviet efforts and resources were devoted to the European front, where the objective was to reduce the influence of the Western powers and replace it with Soviet dominance. The USSR considered the Arab Middle East an area of low expectations. This certainly made sense in view of the fact that by 1947 it had undergone diplomatic defeat in Iran, Turkey, and Greece—areas much more important to Soviet national interests at the time than the Arab Middle East.

The Soviet expectation of ideological support from Jewish socialism in the new state of Israel was almost immediately torpedoed by an unexpectedly sharp conflict. This conflict arose over Israel's *aliyah* demands in the face of unexpected Soviet sensitivity to the possibility of domestic political upheavals resulting from the divisiveness of ethnic identity. The Soviet Union underestimated the vital importance the emigration of Jews from Russia had in the political culture of the new Jewish state. On the other hand, Israel grossly underestimated Soviet sensitivity to interference in Soviet domestic affairs as exemplified in the Jewish emigration demands.

Israel's stand on Korea proved to the Soviets that the Communists (or pro-Soviet leftists) in Israel would not be a decisive factor in setting Israeli national policy.

After the death of Stalin, a new Soviet Middle East policy gradually evolved. It should be noted that the movement toward the Soviet-Arab entente was not due to Soviet initiative alone. Most of the Arab states were readily willing to disassociate themselves from Western defense designs, while Israel, at times, was indecisive. Western political values also proved much more attractive to Israel.

At first the Anglo–Egyptian Treaty of October, 1954, was viewed with apprehension by Moscow, inasmuch as it might serve as the foundation for pro-Western leanings on the part of Nasser's Egypt. This proved not to be the case. On the contrary, the Soviet alignment with the Arab states was largely due (1) to the West's willingness to abandon Nasser for success in creating a Middle East containment alliance against potential expansion by Russia, and (2) to the Soviet Union's willingness to turn against Israel—in line with Arab ideology strongly dedicated to the elimination of Israel from the Middle East.

By the mid-1950s, the Soviets had rebuilt their war-shattered economy, had broken the Western atomic weapons monopoly, and were on their way to achieving a nuclear weapons delivery system. The Stalin era was history by 1954. In 1955 the Baghdad Pact came into being—a development which was exceedingly distasteful to Moscow; this, perhaps more than anything else, developed common interests between Egypt and the USSR, and to achieve and maintain friendship with Nasser made it almost imperative to be antagonistic toward Israel.

At the "Big Four" summit conference in Geneva, July, 1955, the Middle East didn't even rate as an agenda item. Within a matter of months the region would become the main arena of the cold war. Given the political configuration of Middle East politics in the prevailing bi-polar world, we may, in retrospect, speculate as to why the Soviet reversal of policy had not occurred sooner, considering the opportunities available in the Mossadeq upheavals in Iran in 1951–53, the "Black Saturday" confrontation in Egypt (January 26, 1952), and the Nasser coup against King Farouk (July 23, 1952).

In any case, the Geneva Summit produced a relaxation of East-West tensions in central Europe, which became known as the "Geneva spirit." This landmark of Soviet diplomacy

'PEACE PIPE'

Burck in The Chicago Sun-Times

Jacob Burck, in The Chicago Sun-Times, *caricatures the Baghdad Pact by depicting its members smoking the Middle East "bubble pipe" of peace.*

reflected a Kremlin decision to ease the expansionist pressure in Europe. It would serve to cover the Soviet flank on the European front to allow for a determined thrust of diplomatic expansion in the Middle East and other third world areas.

The most effective means available at this time for expansion in the Middle East was to side with the Arabs. Israel, once established, could not be subverted from within; and its liberal social organization, coupled with its strong attachment to the Jewish community in the United States, made it impossible for the Kremlin to squeeze any more Soviet national interests out of Israel. On the other hand, Egypt, with Nasser's effective claim to leadership of the Arab nationalist movement, was now most important. Nasser was exceedingly antagonized by the West's use of the Baghdad Pact to cast him aside and break up the Arab unity movement; and, as stated before, Egypt's antagonism was shared, for a different reason, by the Soviet Union. The Soviets were not long in realizing that "to love Nasser meant to hate Israel."

The bloody Israeli "retaliatory raid" against the Egyptian military outpost in Gaza, only four days after the creation of the Baghdad Pact, created additional opportunities for the Soviet Union in the Middle East. Politically, Nasser could not afford to ignore the Israeli act. It called forth a renewed effort on the part of Egypt to find a source for arms. Negotiations with the Western powers for military equipment became hopelessly protracted as a result of political differences— Western demands upon Egypt which Nasser, particularly after the Bandung Conference, found unacceptable. In the end, Egypt secretly reached an arms agreement with the Soviet Union which represented a mutual payoff for the interests of both states, but which created problems for the entrenched Western interests and objectives in the Middle East. In an effort to salvage whatever remained of Western possibilities in this new reality, the United States, as spokesman for the West, made a formal offer (December 17, 1955) to finance the Aswan Dam. Yet by this time, Nasser's success had inflated his assumed bargaining strength much beyond what the West was willing to accept in the negotiating arena.

NEW HABITAT FOR A BEAR

In early fall, 1955, the Russian bear took some big steps into the Middle East. (Reprinted with permission from the Minneapolis Tribune)

By the end of 1955, therefore, the Soviet Union had made considerable gains in the Middle East by the new pro-Arab, anti-Israel formula—the Soviet Middle East policy had almost turned the proverbial "hundred and eighty degrees" in supporting the Arab states (with the exception of Iraq) against Israel. The dramatic events of 1956 completed the reversal and made the radical Soviet policy switch in the Middle East more obvious. The French, British, and Israeli invasion of Egypt was the momentous event which sealed the Soviet policy. Israel was motivated by the increased threat from an energized Egyptian military supplied with sophisticated weapons; Britain was motivated by its frustration associated with the nationalization of the Suez Canal by "that new dictator on the Nile;" and France wanted to "even the score" with Nasser for aiding the Algerian rebels, as well as threatening access to Middle East oil via the Suez Canal.

The abrupt American cancellation of finances for the Aswan Dam (July 19, 1956) triggered the Egyptian nationalization. The American offer had always been considered in terms of certain responsibilities on Egypt's part. In Dulles' view, these responsibilities included a minimum of goodwill toward the West; a reduction of aid, trade, and technical assistance agreements with the Soviet Union; and the easing of antagonism toward Israel. More specifically, after Egypt's recognition of Communist China, and the pro-Soviet emphasis in the June 18 celebrations terminating the British military presence in Egypt, the United States decided Nasser had failed "to deliver"—Nasser had failed to deliver on a minimum of American expectations. U.S. domestic politics also played a role; this was an election year, and Congress was in no mood to appropriate tax money for a Nasser who seemed to go out of his way to excessively criticize the United States. He was becoming an increasingly negative image in the minds of the American voter, and this carried influence as the Congress prepared to face the electorate in November.

These ten years, 1947–1956, were a crucial decade for international politics in the Middle East. In this decade the Soviets instituted a major policy revision in their relationship to the historic strategic crossroads of three continents. Soviet policy in the Middle East showed that the Western Democracies had no monopoly on the proverbial "muddling through." Soviet policy was a combination of ideological objectives, strategic priorities, and tactical maneuvering, together with the death of Stalin and other chance occurrences. Moscow played "the game of nations" in the Middle East arena with Marxist–Leninist principles, but also with obvious Soviet national interests—traditional and pragmatic—clearly visible. The Middle East was essentially a side show in which low risk gains were measured against the top priority goals located in central Europe. Only after informal understandings had defused the confrontation in Europe in the mid 1950s, a new leader had emerged in the Kremlin, and the British presence was on the way out of the Middle East did the Soviets intensify policy moves there. This new thrust was exemplified by Moscow breaking the Western arms monopoly against Egypt; supporting, with calibrated enthusiasm, Arab national leaders like Nasser; and overtly turning against Israel.

INDEX